Behind Blue Eyes

"No One knows what it's like to be the sad man behind blue eyes."
The Who

BEHIND BLUE EYES:

THE BIOGRAPHY OF DAVID ANTHONY KENNEDY

GRAHAME BEDFORD

davidanthonykennedy.com

Copyright © 2012 by Grahame Bedford. The book author retains sole copyright to his contribution to this book.

All efforts have been made to credit the copyright owners of the photographs.

Bedford, Grahame
Behind Blue Eyes: the Biography of David Anthony Kennedy
ISBN: 978-1475281514
Includes bibliographic references.
Kennedy, David Anthony Kennedy, 1955-1984.
Kennedy Family.

Front cover photo: David Kennedy talks to his mother Ethel at the 1976 Democratic National Convention, © Budrys / Chicago Tribune

SECOND UPDATED VERSION

Behind Blue Eyes

CONTENTS

PROLOGUE	7
PART 1: A CHILDHOOD APART	11
1. ORIGNS	
2. BOBBY'S CONSTANT SHADOW	
3. HE'S A SLICK ONE	
4. NIGHTMARE BECOMES REALITY	
5. BUOYS IN A STORM	
6. THE DEATH OF CAMELOT	
PART 2: DEEPER & DOWN	43
7. EVERY MAN FOR HIMSELF	
8. PAM	
9. NASHVILLE THEN HARVARD	
PART 3: WITH A ROLL OF THE DICE	75
10. NASHVILLE '75	
11. THE PULL OF THE UNDERTOW	
PHOTO SECTION 1	**82-91**
12. THE LOST SON FINDS ENGLAND	
13. NEW YORK CITY 1979	
14. HARLEM BUST AND INTERVENTION	
PART 4: REGAINING HIS BALANCE: SACRAMENTO YEARS	125
15. LIVING IN EXILE: DON JUHL 1980	
16. LIFE IN THE RIVER CITY	
PART 5: FALTERING STEPS	143
17. BACK TO BOSTON	
18. 1984	
PHOTO SECTION 2	**168-177**
PART 6: FINAL DAYS: Easter 1984	179
AFTERMATH	215
EPILOGUE: DEATH BE NOT PROUD	219
APPENDIX: TRIVIA	225
BIBLIOGRAPHY	226

Behind Blue Eyes

PROLOGUE
CALIFORNIA JUNE 4, 1968

The day remained vivid in David's mind. Skies were a foreboding grey and a strong wind whipped up a choppy swell. David and six of his siblings were with their parents in Malibu as Senator Robert F. Kennedy campaigned for the democratic nomination for president.

The day had begun with dreams of better things to come for the United States, but ended in a nightmare with lives shattered - none more than David's, Bobby and Ethel's shy, sensitive third son. He was just days away from becoming a teenager, an important milestone in a young life. But there was something different about the boy that people were unable to pin down. Although bright and good looking, young David appeared to look at life through a different prism. The hues and contours were only making sense to him.

The family's golden child had entered into American royalty. A world in which money, power and success appeared to come together seamlessly. The expectations were enormous. To whom much is given, much is required; David and his contemporaries would recite it on cue. Problem was, as David later observed, "we had all expectation and no guidance." The burden seemed to overwhelm young David.

Even at such a tender age, the word "troubled" which would later come to hang around his neck like an albatross, was already being fixed to his name. There was a depth to his emotional world uncommon in the Kennedy male offspring. There was much going on that was not being communicated. RFK saw this and it worried him. David was the child he had to work the most with he would tell people.

Following his Uncle Jack's assassination in 1963, young David would be assailed by nightmares of his own father's death. One family friend described David as being his father's "constant shadow" following the President's murder. He was the only one of the RFK's not enthusiastic about his father's candidacy in 1968. He feared the worst would happen just like in his dream.

Pop! Pop! Pop! The sound of gunfire would shatter young David's dream. An assailant pounces on his dad out of nowhere. Like his muted, wheel-bound grandfather, Joseph P. Kennedy, he remains a voiceless spectator to the horror unfolding in his nightmare. Next, he sees his father lying motionless on the ground like an old black-and-white news reel. The only color coming from a pool of blood spilling out in a widening circle under the back of Bobby's head. He is not conscious. He wakes with his heart pounding in a cold sweat, mixed with bitter tears.

Every night the same scenario. RFK, recognizing himself thirty years before, was especially cognizant of the boy's needs and special sensitivities. Their bond was easy to see - Bobby was the anchor in David's life; the constant, supportive force. That anchor however, had started to slip with David's parents away from home frequently campaigning.

The youngster had recently gotten into strife for a rock throwing incident, which embarrassingly made the papers. Clearly David was missing his dad's presence. Bobby, as a result, had been conscious of bringing his fourth born along with him as much as possible thereafter. David had been allowed to leave school early to head to California with several of his siblings. He would witness his nightmare come to fruition up close.

The RFK's had spent a frenetic couple of days campaigning throughout California in a desperate bid to claim the state's enormous delegate count. California was the ball game, RFK had stated. Lose here and it was all over. He had achieved the unfortunate distinction of being the first Kennedy to lose an election when he went down to defeat in the Oregon primary the previous week.

On Primary day, June 4, the RFK's emerged after having a late sleep in at the Malibu beach house of filmmaker John Frankenheimer. After pushing himself to the point of physical collapse, Bobby was looking refreshed and confident today. The general mood was optimistic. The media capturing a relaxed, casual RFK. Suddenly the impossible dream seemed achievable after all.

In the afternoon, as he talked strategy with his advisors on the beach, RFK kept a close watch on his brood, who were playing in the water. Trouble and strife never seemed so far away.

Without warning, David got caught in an undertow. Struggling in vain against the power of the sea, David felt himself being pulled farther out in the deeper ocean. He desperately tried to get his father's attention.

His last recollection was of being submerged in the soupy gloom of the ocean. In what felt for David like minutes, but in reality, no more than a few anxious moments, Bobby had quickly and decisively saved the boy. But the force of the briny sea had come to close claiming his life.

As David recaptured his breath from the safety of the dry land, his father calmly reprimanded him for getting in too deep. But it was hardly a scolding. RFK had been that boy too. He understood only too well that perpetually striving against older, stronger brothers had characterized much of his early life. Physical daring in order to prove oneself had almost been a rite of passage for the Kennedy males.

As the RFK party prepared to go into LA for the returns, David still shaken by the day's events, reflected on his father's heroism. He felt he needed to demonstrate his gratefulness to his father. He told his dad that he owed his life to him and would look for a way to repay the debt he felt he had to him.

At the Ambassador hotel in LA later that evening, David found himself drawn into the excitement of what would clearly be a decisive win for Bobby in the Californian primary. Bobby was on his way.

The buzz emanating from the fifth floor suite was palpable. David, going largely unnoticed, saw the barely controlled pandemonium of hotel staff, advisors, friends, press and various hangers-on. The party was well under way.

Later as the younger children went to bed, David was determined to stay up and watch his dad's speech on TV. He was given permission to do so as long as kept the sound down low.

After what was regarded as his best speech of the campaign, RFK left the podium for a press conference and momentarily disappeared. A couple of minutes later, screams started to emerge from the hotel's pantry. Confusion soon morphed into full blow panic as the unthinkable had occurred yet again.

TV cameras suddenly appeared disorientated and jerky. When they steadied, David saw his Uncle Steve Smith at the podium asking for medical assistance and trying unsuccessfully to clear the room. A spasm of fear rippled through the boy's stomach. His nightmare had come to pass. He realized he would never have the opportunity to return the life-saving favor of earlier to his father.

Now the golden haired boy of the family would grow to become the black sheep of the Kennedy family. Bobby Kennedy wasn't the only one not to recover from the events of June 4, 1968. For much of the remainder of his life - nearly 16 years - David still felt as if he was trapped in that Malibu undertow, struggling for firm footing, swimming against the tide of the family, searching for the safety of their recognition, but seemingly just out of reach.

While his own life was to be largely misunderstood, there was much that was never written - his many strengths being overlooked in the process. He was always more than a tragic headline or footnote to the family's ill-fortune. There was indeed a fascinating, complex man behind blue eyes.

# PART 1: A CHILDHOOD APART
1955 - 1969

1. ORIGINS

"It's not easy being a child of Camelot – to have your every move, wrong ones especially – grist for publicity. Harder yet, to be bequeathed a legacy of great expectation."
David Kennedy

David Anthony Kennedy was born on June 15th, 1955 in Washington D.C. at 6:20 a.m. the fourth of what would be 11 children. He was his mother's first caesarean section and it was she who suggested his patron saint - Anthony of Padua, responsible for the recovery of lost articles. He came into the world at a time of considerable prosperity, for both sides of his family and the country. It had been ten long years since the end of the Second World War and America was booming. The family into which David was born was on the rise again after a period of tremendous adversity. His Aunt Rosemary had vanished into institutionalized care following a lobotomy in 1940; Uncle Joe Jr had perished in WW2 due to a plane accident as did his Aunt Kathleen in 1948.

His maternal line, the Skakels, though lesser known, shared marked similarities to the Kennedys. There was the considerable financial clout, numerous Catholic offspring and a reckless disregard for rules. There were also fatal plane crashes, including both of David's grandparents shortly after his birth. Problems with the bottle, dysfunctional relationships, a love of the outdoors and practical jokes were also features of the family. There was no escaping the strength of the Skakel genes for the offspring of Bobby and Ethel.

David's maternal grandfather, George Skakel (1892-1955) had built up one of the largest private companies in the U.S. And like Joe became a millionaire by the time he was thirty. His business acumen was said to be unmatched. The depression existed for neither side of David's family.

David's maternal grandmother Ann Brannack (circa 1892-1955) was responsible not only for her daughter Ethel's fierce religious convictions, but also many of the RFK's tall, big boned characteristics. Towering over her husband George at just under 6 foot, the fair haired Ann would succumb to the demon drink too.

By the mid 1950s, David's grandfather, Joseph P. Kennedy (1888-1969) had emerged from his cocoon of grief. The former Ambassador to Great Britain and Wall Street manipulator was the driving force behind the family's enormous wealth (said to be several hundred million dollars, even in his own lifetime) and political ambitions. He seemed to be forever pushing his three surviving sons, Jack, Bobby and Teddy to heights he knew he was unable to attain himself. Jack, even at just 38, had a national profile as a Senator. Whispers of a possible presidential run in 1960 had begun circulating.

David's father, Robert, universally known as Bobby to friend and foe alike, was a 29 year-old graduate of Harvard and the University of Virginia Law School. He was just starting out professionally and still had not formed an exact blueprint of his future. He was mediocre academically, but had many strengths at his disposal. One of which lay in his organizational skills – his management of political campaigns were second to none. Said to be most like his father in temperament, but more like his mother, Rose Fitzgerald in appearance, he exhibited many qualities David himself would show. The shy, small third son in a large boisterous family, Bobby had an enormously difficult time asserting himself. He was introspective and withdrawn but had an explosive temper when pushed too far. He was prone to moments of brooding intensity. There was much similarity in Bobby's unruly hair and general sloppiness in David. Bobby eventually grew a hardened shell to protect his vulnerability, accessible only to those closest to him. David's sensitivity however, would remain painfully raw and exposed.

Bobby began dating Ethel Skakel in 1948, through his sister Jean, best friend and roommate of Ethel at Manhattanville College in Harlem. The twenty-year old Ethel was considerably more outgoing, but shared many traits with David's father. Her enthusiastic love of sport and her fierce competitiveness made her well suited to the rough and tumble of the Kennedys. She hated losing as much as Bobby did. She appeared to be in a blur of activity day and night. Never a great student, Ethel harbored no great personal ambitions for herself outside of being a wife and mother. Her yearbook at Manhattanville said of her: "An excited hoarse voice, a shriek, a pearl of screaming laughter, the flash of shirttails, a tousled brown head – Ethel! Her face is at one moment a picture of utter guilelessness and at the next alive with mischief."

The marriage of Bobby and Ethel took place in June 1950 thus cementing one of the great partnerships. Historian and Kennedy family insider, Arthur Schlesinger Jr says "her enthusiasm and spontaneity delighted him. Her jokes diverted him. Her social gifts offset his abiding shyness. Her inextinguishable gaiety lightened his times of moodiness and pessimism. Her passion moved him. Her devotion offered him reassurance and security...She awakened his sympathy and his humor and brought him out emotionally. Ethel gave him unquestioning confidence, unquenchable admiration, unstinted love."

By the time of David's arrival, the fourth of the brood, Bobby was chief counsel of the Senate Investigations subcommittee. He had just been named as one of the ten most outstanding young men of 1954. His profile was on the rise, despite the unglamorous work of the committee. He had managed his Brother Jack's successful Senatorial campaign of '52. Although he was still cutting his teeth politically, he was a quick study and his capacity for hard work appeared to know no bounds. Yet to reach his thirtieth birthday, a bright future seemed almost a given.

On July 27th, 1955, when David was 6 weeks old both his parents flew to Soviet Central Asia for a two-month long trip of the socialist world. David was left in the care of hired help back home.

The central focus of David's childhood was the estate in Mclean, Virginia called Hickory Hill. The 5 acre, 2 and half story property was originally owned by General George McClellan, who used the manor as his civil war headquarters. JFK bought the property from Supreme Court justice Robert Jackson in 1953 for $125,000. Following Jackie's 1956 miscarriage, the house become too much for them and sold it to the RFK's for the original purchase price. It would remain Ethel Kennedy's primary residence until she put the estate on the market nearly fifty years later. It remained unsold for 5 years with the unidentified buyer eventually paying $8.25 million – in December 2009 down from the original asking price of $25 million.

The rolling hills and wooded acreage was perfect for the RFK'S bourgeoning brood. The grounds had stables, tennis courts and a swimming pool. The white quasi-Georgian mansion had high ceilings, white woodwork, and crystal chandeliers. Additions were made as the years passed. These included an old stone barn which was used as a playhouse, a whole new north wing was built, a living room family room and a pool house all added to the comforts of Hickory Hill. Various assortments of animals with equally varying temperaments roamed the ground.

Writer George Plimpton summed up the scene: "The house stood back from the road up a steep incline, with a steep U-shaped driveway that went up past the front door and was always choked with cars. When they had the big affairs, the cars were parked for a hundred yards along Chain Bridge Road. The guests would walk through the house onto the back terrace and see the tables set down the hill by the swimming pool. You'd get a drink on the terrace and amble down past the big hickory that had a swing hanging down from one of the high boughs, and a tree house in which there was usually a Kennedy child watching you go by, owl-like, with grave, proprietary eyes."

One incident illustrates this very well. One her first day of employment as Ethel's PA at Hickory Hill, Noelle Bombardier (then Fell), was being shown the grounds of the estate when Noelle saw a sign that caught her eye. "Trespassers Will Be Eaten." "My Boy David put that there," Ethel said proudly. "It's pretty funny don't you think?"

The ensuing chaos of Hickory Hill wasn't unlike that of the Skakel home a generation earlier. A near anarchistic scene developed: little order or discipline, kids on the go from morning to night in a virtual free-for-all, and people coming and going. The bedlam was barely controlled during Bobby's lifetime, following his death it became a very different environment.

For the time being however, David grew up in a free-spirited, rambunctious atmosphere, where he was able to pursue all the normal boyhood pastimes and then some.

At the beginning of autumn 1960, five-year-old David began his education at Our Lady of Victory, a Catholic school in Georgetown, DC (though he changed to the Potomac School before his elementary education was complete). His two eldest brothers were already enrolled there - although they soon ended up at the integrated Quaker's Sidwell Friends school also at Georgetown. His sister Kathleen attended a Sacred Heart school - Stone Ridge in Bethesda, Maryland

Photographer Jacques Lowe, who captured many evocative photos of the Kennedys during the 50s and 60s, David included, well remembered his inaugural visit to Hickory Hill.

"I remember the first night coming to dinner, having spent the day with Robert on Capitol Hill," Lowe said. "They had five children then and had recently bought Hickory Hill. I had known Robert for some time in my role as a magazine photographer covering the up-and-coming investigator. He had been sober and serious, revealing sudden flashes of humor and sometimes anger; but I was not prepared for the man I met on coming to the house late that night. All of his reserve seemed to melt in the glory of his family, and the long, difficult day was forgotten in the warmth of love of a father for his children and vice versa. It was chaos, with all the children talking at once and Bobby answering each one of them with humor and sometimes trying to be stern, at which he didn't fully succeed. Ethel instantly accepted this stranger into the house, and later on I had to go upstairs to say to the evening prayers with the children, which took place after a family pillow fight."

As the presidential race drew to its final stages late in the autumn of 1960, Bobby found he had a Nixon supporter among the ranks - young David. The five-year-old told visiting newsmen that he was supporting his Uncle Jack's rival Republican Richard Nixon. "Now, David," Ethel chided him in front of a reporter. "You know you don't mean that!" "Yes I do," the boy said. He insisted until his mother made it clear that she had had enough. "Alright then - Kennedy," David said in surrender.

The succession of Jack Kennedy to the presidency in 1960 propelled the family into the global spotlight. With Bobby now installed as his brother's Attorney General and right hand man, Hickory Hill became the residence of the new frontier. No weekend would be complete without by the elite of Washington stopping by. And no new frontiersman could hold honorary status until he was pushed, fully clothed, into the swimming pool.

Collier and Horowitz write: "The country had seen these wind-swept, photogenic faces at different stages of development and watched their growth and change as if by time-lapse photography. They were, as one journalist had remarked, "America's children." The importance outsiders attached to being a Kennedy amused them. They gawked back at the tourists who peeked through the hedges at Hyannis. Asked what it meant to be a Kennedy, Bobby's son David had once replied, "It means that we're exactly the same as everybody else - except better."

David and the other Kennedy kids would sell so called "Kennedy sand" for a dollar a bag to curious tourists and for a quarter answer Kennedy questions.

2. BOBBY'S CONSTANT SHADOW

Despite Bobby's role as number 2 man in Washington, he always gave as much time as he could to his third son. "I remember vividly David holding onto his father and hugging him a lot," Barbara Kirby recalled. "When the Attorney General came home from his office late in the evening and we were downstairs watching television in the study, it was David who immediately went to sit in his lap." A family friend said, "Bobby's youngsters were always around him, but David was his constant shadow."

"Bobby was beyond belief," Ethel said in an interview. "He really did expend a superhuman effort. I can remember that before going to work he would be out there just tossing the football from 7 to 7:30 every morning. There's a wonderful photograph of it.

"He never missed a football game," she continued. "When he was with the children, he was so involved with them. He made a terrific point of being home with them at dinner."

"There was some level on which David tapped his father's sensitivity," Chuck McDermott said. "You would find him walking with David or with his arm around David. David just seemed to need it."

Bobby playfully teased David about his lisp and affinity with flowers. "Say 'My sister Courtney blows her whistle,'" Bobby would demand. And fake a grimace when David responded with, "My sisther Courtneyth blowth her whisthle."

Larry Newman knew David since he was 6 years old and saw that the central force in his life was his father. "David was the closest one to Bobby," Newman said. "Bobby was the third son and so was David. Both were the runts of the litter. David sort of felt he was the third man out.

"As a young child, David was interested in wild flowers," Larry O'Brien said. "He'd be out in the field gathering dandelions, while the rest of the family engaged in a murderous game of touch football. His father would gently chide him about it, as would his brothers and sisters."

Bobby would see David being bullied and sensed his third son being cast as the runt of the litter, as he himself had been a generation earlier. Bobby even arranged for boxing lessons, telling David, "Don't let anyone buffalo you. Learn how to fight back and learn how to win."

Despite efforts to try and toughen him up, David's sensitivity and emotionalism emerged as a trait very early on. Childhood friends remember him crying a lot and the tenderness with which his father dealt with the tears. When David would collapse in an emotional heap, Bobby would gently remind him that Kennedys don't cry. David would howl even more until his father held him.

Other characteristics surfaced too. He was regarded as the family's best athlete – quick and graceful and developed a sharp mind. His wonderful sense of fun and humor drew lots of friends to him. A family friend says he was always "a bundle of charisma. If he wasn't the most popular kid in the group, you knew he could be by the next week."

Of his male siblings, he was closest to Bobby Jr, less than 18 months his senior. It didn't take them long to develop a reckless derring do. "The boys went into the woodlands after school and hurled black walnut 'grenades' at each other," Laurence Leamer writes. "David and Bobby jr built tall walls made of bales of hay and ordered little Michael to jump off. He did so with aplomb; no matter how high they piled the bales...David came swinging down out of an ancient Hickory Hill tree on a rope. "I'm batman!!" he yelled as he chased after Bobby jr and Michael."

Even Ethel sensed something special about her fourth born. He was arguably the best looking of the RFK's, and his blonde good looks made him something of the golden-haired boy, quite literally.

"If we ever go broke," His mother once said, "we'll make a movie star out of David and live off his earnings."

Though the Camelot era ended violently and abruptly on November 22nd, 1963, David was protected from its full impact, unlike the period following his father's murder. However, when he was picked up from school that late autumn afternoon, without being told, he had somehow worked out what had happened. "Jack's hurt," he announced to the driver, while dialing numbers on his toy phone. "Why did someone shoot him?"

As speculation mounted as to Bobby's future post JFK, life at Hickory Hill continued. Chris Lawford says that the ten-year old David "was small for his age with freckles covering a face that was all innocent trouble. David was like Tom Sawyer. He looked like an angel, but if you weren't careful he'd get you to whitewash the fence for him."

One of the characteristics that he would utilize in later years was an ability to never give up on himself. Chris Lawford describes David's tenacity, saying that the Hickory Hill boxing matches showcased his cousin's courage. It appears he made full use of the boxing lessons he received.

"David might have looked like the ninety-eight-pound weakling in need of a meal," Lawford writes, "but he had the heart of a pissed-off lion. He was tough and tenacious, taking enormous punishment with never a thought of surrendering.

"First up were the two Bobbys – Shriver and Kennedy – who would beat the shit out of each other gracelessly while David and I watched from the sidelines, waiting our turn," Lawford continued. "I sat next to my best friend feeling the nervous dread of waiting my turn to do something I didn't want to do but was powerless not to do. The only thing worse than a coward was a coward who didn't try."

The bout between David and Chris received quite a build up, with RFK even enlisting a trainer for David. "They fought each other more fiercely than family I've ever seen," a former aide to Ted Kennedy thought. "The insults are more cutting, and the put-downs more withering. Yet they'll wipe out an insider who tries to do the same, who dares to seek intimacy without their permission, They are tough, tough people."

"They are bullies when you first meet them," Jack Weeks said. "They want to test how far they can go with you and they push you around getting there."

There was more than a little push and shove in the encounter of the cousins. "It was a little unfair," Lawford observed. "David was tiny and I was big and fat, probably twice his size. This was my only solace – through the luck of place in the family hierarchy I got to go up against someone half my size. But appearances can be deceiving. He looked like one of those cartoon characters, his fists whirling at a hundred miles per hour. Moving ever forward with no capability of reverse.

"I felt worse about hitting him than he felt getting hit. He was driven to win, to make his mark on me. He was ruthless and relentless. Jack Walsh couldn't believe it and told anyone who would listen that David was the toughest kid he had ever seen and certainly the toughest in our family."

By all accounts, it was a largely inconclusive result. Chris thought that he had probably won on points, but said that David was the real winner for having lasted the match without ever retreating.

Behind Blue Eyes

It became something of a Saturday ritual. "Who wants to come with me to the office?" Bobby would ask his offspring, engaged in various activities. While his brothers and sisters would vacillate, David would be in the car, ready to go. "Right," he'd tell David. "Let's go to work." David would putter around the office while Bobby worked or chatted with reporters. Sometimes the boy would get bored and restless and start to cry in frustration. As always, Bobby told David very gently not to cry. David would wail even louder until his father comforted him.

Bobby would grant not just his time to his fourth born, but tangible offerings such as extra pocket money and candy that he didn't allow his other children to have.

"His father went out of his way to give him a lot more privileges," Larry Newman said. "He would give him some extra spending money, which he didn't give the others."

"David and Bobby were so close," Ethel said to one her assistants. "They were inseparable. David was small, a runt like Bobby had been. And Bobby just took to him, you know? David was always very sensitive, very introverted," Ethel continued, "not like the other boys. He and I would go and pick flowers while his brothers were killing each other with their crazy games. If he ever got in trouble, he really didn't care what I thought what I thought about it. He cared what Bobby thought. If Bobby was unhappy with him, it was the end of his world."

Childhood friend, Liza Noyes describes David in pre-adolescence as "smart, argumentative, affectionate, sloppy and very funny. His motto was 'do want you want and beg for forgiveness later,'" Noyes Said. "That always got a laugh.

"He pushed me down once during a game of Mawl Ball and I cried a little longer than I really needed to," Noyes recalled. "I was sent to the infirmary, and when the teacher made him apologize, we both blushed.

"Later...he tackled Krikky Rose during a game of British Bulldog and she broke her arm," Noyes said. "When his father came to speak at a school assembly, Krikky got the Senator to sign her cast.

"David was reckless but not malicious," Noyes stated. "He was bewildered that things could go so wrong, that bones could break. I just keep remembering how it felt to hold his thin, little boy's body. He hugged so tight, it hurt sometimes."

"I always felt that David, more than brothers, was his father's son," Chris Lawford added. "He was in the middle of the family: small, fast and elusive. He had a big heart, but was ruthless in its protection and he had a biting sense of humor. He was the one whom Uncle Bobby said was 'the one I have to work with.'

"I remember seeing a picture of David walking with dad in the New York City St. Patrick day Parade," Lawford furthered. "He was dressed in his little suit and overcoat, his mop top hair cut almost hiding his eyes. He was holding his father's hand. There was no mistaking they were father and son. David was the ten-year-old version of his father and in his eyes you could see that wherever his dad led him, it would be just fine."

3. "HE'S A SLICK ONE"

There was time for the usual boyhood mischief as Chris Lawford writes:

"I had finally caught David. It had taken the better part of a half hour and all my wind, but I had him. He was on his back, stuck deep in the squishy chair in Aunt Ethel's living room. We had been fighting our way across the RFKs' house in Hyannis Port room by room, doing little damage but making a hell of a lot of noise.

"I outweighed David by thirty pounds, so if I could catch him I could beat the stuffing out of him. The problem was catching him. He was fast and elusive, with an uncanny instinct for escape. He was like a mosquito buzzing around your head and then disappearing until you felt the bite on your arm or leg. His tactics were to provoke until you couldn't help but go after him; then he would go into his mosquito routine, driving whoever was unlucky enough to be chasing him into a frenzy until they gave up, hoping for a future opportunity when he might let his guard down. David rarely let his guard down.

"David loved to infuriate. He could do it with his speed on the football field or with his intellect and wit. Nobody was spared, except me. I was his best friend and ally. I was also no match for his speed or wit. This didn't mean we didn't fight — but it was usually at long distance.

"Now I was whaling on him, making up for all those times I had come up empty. I had the advantage, but David didn't have the instinct to surrender. He had me by the hair and yelling, "Chris Lawford's beating me up. Help! Get him off me. Help." I couldn't figure out who he thought might help him. There wasn't anyone who didn't think this whupping wasn't long overdue.

"Well, maybe there was one person.

"They say a mother's love is blind. And so I found myself in the crosshairs of the Big E. Aunt Ethel, the volatile one, was on her way to his rescue. I could hear her coming. "Chris Lawford, you get off David this minute!"

"This was good enough for me. My hands flew up into the air in the universally recognized sign of surrender. I knew better than to cross the Big E. We had all tried and it never worked out too well.

"I had my hands in the air and my head buried deep in David's chest because he still had large clumps of my hair clutched in his hands. If there was one thing that my best friend knew how to do, it was take advantage of an opportunity...you could be damn sure that if he found himself with his adversary's hands in the air, rendered impotent by his rescuing mother, he'd start hitting me in the face with his right while he pulled my hair out of my head with his left, which he did.

"It must have looked to the Big E like I was still whaling on her son, because when she got to us, she grabbed my hand with such force that she broke my thumb with a snap. This got my attention fast got me off David, who sat back and laughed."

The day Bobby entered the 1968 presidential race, St. Patrick's Day, was a life changing moment for David also. "David didn't want his father to run for president," Larry Newman said. "They'd ask him why, and he said because he would be shot like his Uncle John."

David was the lone dissenter in the family, strongly arguing against his dad's candidacy. "I was shaken when Daddy ignored us and ran," David said later. He would be assailed by nightmares about his father that seemed like premonitions. "His father reassured him but David never lost his fear," Chris Lawford said.

With his parents away, David was developing a growing reputation as a trouble maker. On the night of April 12, 1968, Hickory Hill neighbor, Jack Kopson had had enough. For weeks he had been tormented by David and his siblings and cousins with cherry bombs and firecrackers spewing debris across his lawn. After an incident on this particular night, Kopson raced outside and fired a shotgun blast at the ground - missing David by a hare's breath.

"I didn't want to hurt him, just scare him and his two older brothers from coming around my place," Kopson later said. But the mischief continued. "Mrs. Kennedy ought to come on home and watch her children instead of traipsing all over Indiana," Kopson declared at the time. "There is no upbringing over there. No one is controlling those kids."

Kopson arranged for his son-in-law to wait nearby in a truck and observe David and his cohorts - he was determined to nab them. David was duly caught and hauled into the Kopson home. He appeared calm and unflappable.

"David Kennedy was the spokesman for the group," Kopson said. "He denied everything. He's a slick one. He said they had been hearing about mailboxes being ruined." Kopson's attempts to contact Ethel fell on deaf ears.

His trouble making continued and soon made the news - just as voters were heading to the polls in Indiana. On Saturday, April 27, while his father was campaigning, David got into trouble for throwing stones at passing cars on a highway near Hickory Hill. Missing his father's special attention, he and a friend had gotten into strife while unsupervised. One driver, Leo Correa had his windscreen shattered and brought the matter before the Washington police. Bobby issued a statement from Indiana. "I regret to say that one of my sons in the company of another boy got into trouble last Saturday while my wife and I were away from home. He feels very badly about what he has done and has apologized to all concerned. He is a good boy who has always been a source of joy and pride to all our family and never has been involved in any trouble whatsoever prior to this incident. He and Mrs. Kennedy will of course appear at the appropriate time and place to meet the requirements of the law."

The matter was dropped after the Kennedys paid the $119.72 to have Correa's windscreen replaced.

"David was chided and ridiculed by the Senator and Mrs. Kennedy, but not for what he did," Bob Galland said later. "The Senator and Mrs. Kennedy felt Dave was stupid to get caught. I think the Senator took Dave aside and they had a chat while the Senator was putting on a suit getting ready to go somewhere, but that was it."

Remembering those days twenty-five-years later, Galland said, "David was the one always getting into trouble, whether it was of his own doing, or he got blamed by the other kids." But Galland felt that all of the Kennedy youngsters were problems. "Their philosophy was, 'Let's see what we can get away with.'"

"There was always something or other," said a reporter who covered RFK's presidential campaign. "He sort of got lost in that big crowd of kids, but we knew that David was the one who was always being hauled in by the police."

Despite the difficulties that arose from his parents' absences, "David had a great sense of wonderment," Laurence Leamer observed. "He had an awareness of the world around him far beyond his twelve years. On the cusp of adolescence, David was old enough to realize that the Kennedy name was a magic wand that he could wave to get what he wanted - and that all was not right with himself and his family. When his father descended on David's life, he gave a rapid-fire quiz on history and current affairs over lunch, or sent a football spiraling toward David in an invisible end-zone."

4. NIGHTMARE BECOMES REALITY

David finished the seventh grade at the Potomac School early so he could accompany his father and some of his siblings in California for the primary schedule for June 4. It would be an eerie few days for David as several strange events occurred that would markedly change his life.

There was even drama before David had left the airport. Ethel recounts the incident. "We sent the top four out to California on their own to go skiing," she said to a journalist at the time. "They were supposed to call the minute they landed at the San Francisco airport. That should have been at eleven. By twelve I was pacing; by one everybody was going mad. At two, the phone rang. It was Kathleen, who said, 'It's o.k. you can stop worrying about David.' I yelled, 'David!' And then Kathleen explained calmly that they'd left him at the airport. He was fine – He just sat right there waiting for them to remember him."

Primary day arrived at the John Frankenheimer house where David, his parents and five siblings were staying and sleeping late. Little could David of known of the extraordinary events to take place over the next 18 hours. Following a leisurely breakfast, David and some of his siblings rushed in and out of the ocean only to be cautioned by their father: there was an undertow in surf; best to wait until he came down to supervise them.

The rest of the morning on the beach was uneventful. At 2 p.m. however there was high drama. The waves had noticeably changed and the pull out to sea was massive. It would be a dangerous time to ignore Mother Nature.

David lost his balance as he tried to catch a wave. A powerful surge took him beneath the foaming surf. He then saw a huge wave about to crash upon him from a tremendous height. He frantically waved his arms in order to draw his father's attention who was talking on the beach. David wasn't sure if Bobby had seen him or not. He remembered yelling, "Help! I can't stand up!" moments before the driving ocean pounded him down to the sandy floor of the ocean.

David's next realization was of strong arms hauling him out of the undertow. His dad had heard his desperate plea for help.

"Let me down!" David demanded, his father smiling gently. He was aware his son was trying to put on a brave face. But death had come close to claiming him, and wasn't finished.

Bobby let his son go who hunched over the sand spluttering and coughing up sea water. His father gently reprimanded him for going beyond his depth, but only gently. Bobby understood what it was like to feel the need to prove oneself physically. He too followed older stronger brothers. As a child himself, RFK had thrown himself into the ocean not much younger than David was in order to learn to swim. Jack Kennedy said later that "It showed a lot of guts or no brains at all, depending on how you looked at."

Journalist Theodore White (1915-1986) best known for his books on the presidential elections 60-72 lunched with the RFK's at the home of film maker John Frankenheimer on the day of the Californian primary. He saw how quickly the conditions became overpowering and all enveloping. Writing for Life magazine, White says, "It was a windy, overcast afternoon. The sea was rough, but the kids were dashing in and out of the water. David went in with his father and suddenly this wave came and just enveloped them. They disappeared beneath the surf for a few anxious moments and when they reemerged Bobby had hold of his son. David was spitting up sea water and Bobby had sustained a cut over his eye..."

Speech writer Richard Goodwin found Bobby stretched out across two chairs motionless. But he was only sleeping. "God," thought Goodwin. "I suppose none of us will ever get over John Kennedy."

"Bobby just jumped right in and saved him," Ethel recalled to Noelle Bombardier, an assistant. "He saved David's life the very same day he lost his own, and David never really could understand any of it. It was as if he thought God had traded his life for his dad's."

Following the frightening incident in the surf, some believe that Bobby's hero status became even stronger in David's eyes. "That seems to have made Bob even larger than life to David," John Seigenthaler believes. "And then 12 hours later, he lost this father in a most horrible way."

David had told his father that he owed him his life and would try to repay him in some way, down the road. But it was not to be.

The RFK entourage had gathered in the Royal Suite on the seventh floor of the Ambassador Hotel in downtown LA for the returns. It became something of an impromptu celebratory cocktail party. It didn't take the group - family members, reporters and the odd hangers- long to get into the swing of things. The drinks flowed, conversation was buoyant, the mood optimistic. It was impossible to underestimate the importance of winning the crucial primary in California. Victory would almost certainly propel Bobby to the democratic nomination in August. It was a jubilant scene in the suite that night. Their man was on his way.

The children were staying in bungalows of the Beverly Hills Hotel but were visiting their parents at the Ambassador. David, dressed in blue blazer and grey slacks, was still excited from playing with a spider monkey from one of Frankenheimer's film sets earlier in the day.

At 11 p.m. Ethel told her 4th born it was time to go to bed, but got permission to watch TV if the sound was low. His dad came in and kissed him good-night and left for victory speech downstairs. David dozed on and off, but finally shook himself awake to make sure he didn't sleep through his dad's victory speech.

At 12:15 a.m. on June 5, RFK had formally accepted victory and had left the dais for a press conference in a nearby room. David, the only RFK offspring still awake, was suddenly alerted to a commotion that was occurring downstairs. He was unaware of what the broadcaster was conveying - but everyone there seemed frantic. David froze in horror as the full impact of the devastating event hit home - he beloved father was shot! He remembered feeling like he couldn't breathe and wondered if he was ever going to – just like after he nearly drowned a few hours earlier.

"...As we were going through the kitchen, Bobby was shot," Ethel told her assistant Noelle Bombardier. "I was standing right there, and this...this...person...killed my husband. "And my son (David) saw the whole thing on TV."

"I really didn't know what was going on – or what to do," David said. "My brothers and sisters were asleep."

"I was in my room all by myself," David told Noelle Bombardier in 1984, shortly before his own death. "All the politicians and grown-ups were downstairs, and I didn't want to go down there, so I stayed in my room. I was watching television and then all of a sudden I saw my dad get shot, and I saw my mother kneeling over him, and I thought, that's it. He's dead. It just plays over and over in my head," he said, "Over and over and over...

"He should have known he was going to be shot," David said angrily. "And he should have cared what that was going to do to us."

"Do you want to know something?" Ethel asked Noelle. "For a moment, I actually thought he would live after he was shot. Why, he opened his eyes, Noelle, and looked right up at me. And I thought, 'My God! He is going to live! But then he closed his eyes. And that was it. He never opened them again."

Bob Galland was the young man left in charge of the RFK brood that night. "There was no doubt the Senator had been shot. David saw it. There was a definite shock there," recalled Galland. "I left the TV on five, seven, ten seconds too long. I'm standing there flipping around to catch other coverage and then just turned the damned thing off. I sat down with David and for a few awkward moments wondered what the hell I was going to say to this kid now. Jesus I gotta do something. So I give him a hug and said, "David, let's just go for a walk for a while, wait and see what happens. Other news reports'll come in." He said something like, "Oh man, it's over...they got him too."

They walked the silent streets for more than an hour before returning to the pool of the Beverley Hills Hotel drinking cokes.

"There were a couple of emotional minutes, there were tears; he brushed a half a dozen of them away and that was it. He was a Kennedy. He handled it like a big boy," recalled

Galland. "I was surprised by his maturity, but he was evidently prepared in his own mind for the worst.

"I could tell that it was definitely something he had wrestled with before. I wanted to know what had happened to the Senator but my responsibility was to David. At 21, I wasn't prepared for this. David was obviously tired, so I left him sitting there and I went into the hotel lobby and told the guy I wanted a room closer to the front desk. I told him who I was and he gave me a key and I got David. He obviously wasn't going to go to sleep and I didn't want him waking the other kids. I stayed with him for a while, got him undressed, and put him to bed and told him if I heard any news I'd be back immediately."

An anxious nation waited, still reeling from the murder of Dr. Martin Luther King just 8 weeks earlier. 25 agonizing hours later, Bobby passed away. His sister Kathleen wrote about the night in a piece for the book "Kennedy: The New Generation."

"He was alone and supposed to be asleep, but the excitement of the day had kept him awake. In the aftermath of the tragedy, it was sometime before someone came to check on him. It was presidential biographer Theodore White who found the boy "devastated at the sight he had just seen.' Without stopping to rationalize why, White ordered a soothing hot chocolate from room service and cradled and comforted the shaken youngster."

Galland walked into the hotel restaurant, where he ran into John and Ann Glenn, who wanted to know how the children were. Glenn, remarkably calm, told Galland, "I just want to make sure I can reassure Ethel that the kids are fine." About that time, Galland recalled, Theodore White, who was working on his book The Making of the President, 1968, also arrived at the hotel. The Glenns, White and another couple tiptoed into David's room and sat in the dark as the boy slept. As Galland remembers it, "They were all hot to go wake up the other kids and I wouldn't let them do that."

Bill Adler thought that David carried a mother lode of guilt about the incident. "David could think only of his own trauma earlier that morning. His father had snatched him from the arms of death with his strength. But death had refused to be thwarted. If it couldn't have the son, it must take the father. It was his fault – he had caused his father to die. Yet he could never tell anyone."

The trauma was not yet over for David. The funeral train carrying his father's body to Arlington Cemetery on June 8 was not without incident.

Collier and Horowitz describe David's dazed state during the trip. He'd barely spoken a word in the past three days.

"For much of the trip to Arlington, he had his head out of the window of the train, letting the wind batter his face. Once, as they were entering a tunnel, Phil Kirby, David's close friend from Hyannis whom Ethel had asked along to keep him company, noticed that David didn't see the protruding arm of a steel girder and yanked him back into the compartment to keep him from being decapitated. Both boys had their heads out the window again when a train running on a parallel track to theirs struck a group of bystanders at a crossing; two people were killed, one of them cut in half under the wheels. David had been mesmerized by the bloody scene, unable to tear himself away until a Secret Service man got him back down in his seat."

Following Bobby's death, Larry Newman saw the pain that David endured. "He was very angry at the world, and he would curse Sirhan Sirhan," Newman recalled. "He said he wanted him to rot in jail forever."

"I saw him on occasions when he was in one of the fits of anger," Newman went on. "When he would curse the assassination and what it did to his life, and then the tears would come and he would run off and the people they hired to watch him would follow him. I think the kid was in pain all the time...He was living this horrible sorrow that never ended."

"In a sense, David stopped growing when his father died," a friend suggested. "He was doomed to never really grow up and mature into a man."

Following his 13th birthday on June 15, which nobody was really up for, David and various family members flew to Connecticut for a river adventure from Mystic to Hyannis Port. Collier and Horowitz:

"Ethel careened between gloom and febrile gaiety all during the trip. Once she took Bobby Jr and David below and hit them repeatedly with a hairbrush, the first such punishment they could remember, and one that made them cry in spite of their teenager resolutions to be stronger than their mother. "I can't stand it anymore," she said when they reached home port. "You guys have got to get away from here." Thus begun a Diaspora that would continue for years to come, a process of leaving and returning that symbolized the next generation's ambiguous tie to the Kennedy Legacy."

5. BUOYS IN A STORM

In July, Ethel sent David with Chris in tow to summer camp at Mayrhofen in Austria. Chris Lawford takes up the story:

"It was the summer of Uncle Bobby's death and a change in our attitude toward everything having to do with being a Kennedy. It was like watching a big balloon lose its air. Things just didn't have much meaning anymore.

"David and I packed our duffel bags and some baggies stuffed with mescaline and pot. We transited through Munich, which was terrifying given our fear of the Germans. The Nazis might have gone, but we didn't want any part of what they'd left behind. Each of us carried our contraband in our underwear and tried to look like the innocent thirteen year olds were weren't.

"We touched down in the heart of the German Republic on a rainy morning in July with our troop of well-heeled, oblivious, aspiring tennis players. As we marched to customs David and I had visions of ending up in some gulag in front of a snarling German Sheppard and a pair of Aryan-filled jackboots.

"Suddenly we became separated from the group. We were alone, but at least we had each other. Then suddenly David was gone. Vanished. One moment he was in line to show his papers to the not-so-nice immigration man and the next he wasn't. I made it through customs and onto the bus, which is when I volunteered to the head counselor, "Excuse me Jeff, but

Behind Blue Eyes

I don't see my cousin David anywhere." Jeff initiated a search as I panicked. I was sure they had caught David, and I wasn't sure whether he would roll over.

"Then from out of nowhere, out popped a disheveled David looking as if he'd just been in a fight.

"David slid into the seat next to me. "Where the fuck did you go, man? I stammered. He gave me one of his looks of disappointment and said, "Thanks for leaving me alone with the Nazis, man!'

"I had no idea what he was talking about, what had happened. We skied and played tennis and screwed girls the entire time we in Austria, maybe not what our moms had in mind when they sent us there.

"Mayrhofen was this quaint Austrian town tucked away in the Alps. In the morning we would ski in shorts and a T-shirt until the snow turned to water; then we'd head to the tennis courts. Not a bad life if you can get it. David and I were a perfect team. He was a great skier and terrible tennis player; I sucked on skis but was good with a racket. But winning didn't seem to matter anymore...David and I decided there really wasn't any reason to try and be good, so we might as well try to be bad.

"We didn't win any sporting awards but both got girlfriends. David lost his virginity to a girl who was 'sorry about what happened to his father.'"

"Some 17 year-old girl at the camp realized who I was and picked me up," David later recalled. "I was hardly into puberty. Chris told me to take her out and try and feel her tits. I did it. All of a sudden she was unzipping my pants and pulling them down and sort of moaning about how bad she felt that my father had died."

When he got back home, David began waiting for someone to talk to him about his father's death. "No one ever talked to me about what I was feeling," David said. "No one ever talked to me about my father's death. To this day, in fact, my mother has never spoken about it." When he finally cornered his mother and asked her about the assassination, she snapped, "It's not a subject I want to discuss" and elbowed her way past the youngster.

While there has been much criticism of Ethel's parenting skills, those close to her have nothing but praise for her in the immediate aftermath of her husband's murder. "If she's downbeat, she never let's on," according to columnist Art Buchwald. "She bounces back; nothing really defeats her," was the comment of another insider.

Though life for David at Hickory Hill would become increasingly difficult, the estate retained much of its original charm. "It has the same zany quality, with 12 things going on at once," a friend reported.

There was a discussion among the children as to whether they should continue to live at Hickory Hill. Shortly after Bobby's death, Ethel told friends "the children are so brave. They have helped me more than they can know." It was the children, in a typical family conference of their own, who decided they wanted to keep Hickory Hill as home. "Old Moms," as Ethel laughingly calls herself, agreed with them.

"David was the most devastated by the death of his father," stated writer Harrison Rainie. "He was the one that reacted most destructively to his pain...He got involved in drugs early on, and he got hooked."

He hung around with his brother Bobby's crowd calling themselves the Hyannis Port Terrors (HPT). Dressed in dark clothes and painting their faces black, the teenagers would sneak out of Ethel's late in the evening for a night of mischief.

"Usually they'd meet three or four other kids in Hyannis and spend the nights causing all sorts of trouble," Thomas Langford remembered. "I was a charter member of the HPTs. Sometimes I played along, when I had the nerve. We'd shoot off firecrackers, deflate people's tires, stick potatoes in the exhaust pipes of cars, turn over trash cans, mess around with girls...all sorts of mischief.

"After we did our bit, Ethel would get calls from everyone in town complaining about it," Langford continued. "At first she used to say, 'My kids were home asleep last night, I don't know what you're talking about.' But one night she waited up, and, sure enough, she caught me, Bobby and David jumping out one of the second-floor windows of her home. She chased us all over the compound in the middle of the night in her nightgown and bare feet, finally losing us somewhere on the stretch of beach. The next morning, the brothers told me they snuck back in the house while she was asleep. But then she got up before they did and locked them both in their bedroom. When she finally let them out at about eight that night, they took off with one her sheets. Apparently during their time alone all day, they'd made a makeshift flag out of it, which had emblazoned on it the words, 'HPT's Rule.' That night they rigged it so that they could get it up on the steeple of a local church, St. Andrew's Presbyterian. I happened to be at Ethel's sitting in the living room the next day watching TV with Bobby Shriver when the doorbell rang."

Upon opening the door, Ethel was confronted by the minster for St. Andrew's with a bedsheet in his hands. When asked what it was, the minster showed her the monogrammed initials RFK. "The next time your boys want to fly a flag, ask them to do so from the steeple of the Catholic Church, not from mine." Closing the door Ethel yelled, "Give me strength!"

Amidst the general hell-raising, David was introduced to drugs by Bobby Jr while still 13. He smoked pot regularly and dropped acid. A neighbor at Hyannis Port, John Kelley remembers the first time David tried drugs, during the autumn of '68. He said that Bobby had laid out some mescaline and dared David to consume it. Another friend, Phil Kirby said "Don't do that David. Please don't do it." He hesitated a moment then popped the pill. He began hallucinating – thinking that the hedgerows had sharp leaves to them, he asked Bobby to move away so he wouldn't be hurt. Bobby moved closer into the bushes and the leaves seem to penetrate his brother's body David said, "You're dying, just like Daddy.

The horrible year that was 1968 came to an end with the RFK children putting a book for their mother memorializing Bobby. David's entry was the stand out – an extraordinary piece for a 13 year-old.

"Daddy was very funny in church because he would embarrass all of us by singing very loud. Daddy did not have a very good voice. There will be no more football with Daddy, no

more swimming with him, no more riding with him and no more camping with him. But he was the best father there ever was and I would rather have him for a father for the length of time I did than any other father for a million years."

In June of 1969 David suffered a broken right arm from a game of touch football at Hickory Hill. He had collided with none other than Redskins lineman Ray Schoenke, who along with teammates, were regular visitors to the McLean estate.

"He pats the cast and tells his friends, 'Ray Schoenke gave me that,'" Ethel told the press.

There were lighter occasions too as the one described by Chris Lawford during the summer of '69, shows:

"David...had a cast on his arm from a break he had suffered a few weeks earlier...In the meantime we devised ingenious coverings for his cast so that he could bodysurf.

David and I convinced "Sandy the surfer" to take us fishing on a Malibu outrigger. It was a small sailboat, meant for one, but we were persistent, so Sandy finally relented and off we went into the deep blue Pacific with two fishing poles and some chopped-up squid. The Kennedys love the ocean...

So "Sandy the surfer" took David and me a mile out into the Pacific on a flimsy boat, two fishing lines hanging off the back with big hunks of squid on them, our legs dangling in the water. I kept my eye on the receding shoreline, saying things like 'maybe we should head in a little.' David was looking to catch something big and figured the farther out we were the more likely it was that would happen.

"He always thoroughly enjoyed my discomfort.

"The shark I was looking at was twelve-feet long and it was circling our boat...I told Sandy it was time to head back. I began reeling my line in with the urgency of a fourteen-year old who didn't want to reprise the fate of those navy sailors I read about bobbing in the South Pacific missing their lower halves. David was looking at things differently; he was going to catch the shark. He yelled at Sandy to sail toward the fins.

'Are you fucking crazy, catching a twelve-foot shark on this boat? If that fish hits your line we are going over.'

Behind Blue Eyes

David grinned his 'I can't believe what a chicken you are' grin and said, 'I don't know why you're getting all dramatic, Chris, it's just a shark.'

He had me and he knew it. 'Just a shark! What are you going to do if you catch it?'

'I'll reel it in!'

'Are you kidding me? Where would you put it if you got it up to the boat?'

David laughed. 'We'll drag it into shore.' Suddenly another fin appeared. Now there were two. Then the first shark disappeared. There were still two, but we didn't know where one of them was. I lost it. All I could imagine was being in the dark cold water at the mercy of something big and unseen below me.

David was thrilled. Now there were two targets. I demanded he bring in his line, losing all pretense of indifference and sounding a lot like one of our mothers. 'David, if you don't reel that line in right now, you can forget about me being your best friend.' He relented, but his disappointment at my cowardice was evident. We were headed into shore, the lines and bait almost out of the water, David using every tactic he could come up with to keep his line in the water as long as possible. It was annoying but expected. I was feeling a lot less panicked, when out of the deep blue sea with squid and hook in mouth appeared the missing twelve-foot thrasher. It was one of those slow motion moments. I happened to be looking right at the spot where the fish broke the surface, six feet from our boat; and when it did, we got wet. I screamed, 'Shit,' at the top of my lungs. David shouted, "I got it." That brought another 'Shit' from me. His duel was short-lived as the shark bit through his line and was gone. In the aftermath of such an encounter there is usually stunned silence followed by a rush of excitement and euphoria in the reliving of the event. So it was with the three of us, although my euphoria was somewhat tempered by the knowledge that I did not have the same penchant for engaging danger as my fearless cousin."

6. THE DEATH OF CAMELOT

As the final summer of the decade was at its midpoint, Teddy's growing recklessness following Bobby's murder had reached its zenith. Always the life of the party, Teddy seemed determined to continue hell-raising, ignoring the call for his last drinks. The final nail in the coffin of Camelot occurred on July 18, 1969 at the now infamous Chappaquiddick Island in Massachusetts. Ted, like many other males in the Kennedy family, had a long history of reckless driving. After a night of partying he mistakenly drove off a bridge and plunged in the water, killing a female passenger, Mary-Jo Kopechne, a staffer of RFK's. The frantic restoration of his political career ensured, that only recovered in the final decade of his life - some thirty years later. Questions of character and conduct abound to this day. For most, the lion of the senate, who himself has passed into history, would remain a flawed giant.

David was appalled. "I don't know what motivated him that night," he said later, "but Teddy's behavior sickened me." It was typical candor and to the point.

"I am sure that if there was any reflection on Ted's part," one of David's friends said to this author, "he would have had to account for this period in his life and that of his charges. How could anyone look up to a person that seemed so out of it all the time? David, I doubt was not the only one who felt this way, but, he was the only one to voice it. Yep, that was David alright, not afraid to speak up but always on the wrong side of the family for doing it." One of David's girlfriends from the mid 70s said he spoke to her about the incident and his private view of the circumstances. "I do not wish to speak badly of Teddy," she said to the author of this book. "I do believe he was a great guy who eventually bore the brunt of his heavy load admirably. I do know he loved David greatly...at least David thought so. Then again, we who loved David...how could you not love him?

"David spoke of the scuttlebutt around the compound after Chappaquiddick. Rumor was Teddy and another woman had left the party. When the accident happened they escaped. They did not know Mary Jo was in the car. No one saved her in time, because no one knew she was there until they returned to the party after the accident. Apparently she had gotten tipsy and went and laid down in the back of the car to sleep/pass out/whatever. I don't know if it is true if this sheds more light on Teddy's action. I guess he was in a no win situation. Mind you this was just a rumor. Those who knew David will no doubt remember he was very intuitive. I feel sure he had no problem latching onto the whispered undertones. For me this view of the accident is much more palatable."

The peaks and troughs continued for the Kennedys. An especially high point - literally - concluded the extraordinary 1960s for David and his family. Jim Whittaker was an old mate of RFK's and the first American to climb Everest. He took Bobby out to climb Mount Kennedy in memory of JFK in 1965. Now a new trip and a new generation beckoned - almost symbolically, their gait considerably less certain or confident. The plan was to climb Mount Rainier, the 14,000 feet (4,000m) summit and invited David and Cousin Chris Lawford along. Lawford describes the adventure, which would make David the youngest ever person to climb the mountain, at just 14.

"David and I flew into the rain of Seattle and were met by Jim, his brother Lou, and Jim's two sons, Carl and Scott. We drove the two hours to Mount Rainier in the anticipation of doing something that would be difficult at best and life-threatening at worst. I had never seen Mount Rainier. It's huge, over fourteen thousand feet high. You know that's high because there's snow all over the top and it's the middle of summer…David was nervous but wouldn't show it. He had a whole association going on with his father's climb of Mount Kennedy fuelling his determination… David just trudged with some kind of inner purpose.

"Once at base camp, which took the entire day to get to…David and I crawled into our tent, exhausted and cold. I was wondering why in the hell I had agreed to this and counting the minutes until I would be off this godforsaken mountain. David was thinking about the summit.

'The summit?' I said. 'Are you fucking kiddin'? Do you hear that wind out there? It will blow your skinny ass right off this mountain and leave me here all alone with the Whitakers.'

'Shut up Chris,' David said. 'I've got to get some sleep. We've got a big day tomorrow.

'A big day tomorrow' – this did not sound like the David Kennedy I knew, the David Kennedy who was negative about anything that could be classified as a 'good thing to do.' Shit, maybe this lack-of-oxygen-affecting-the-brain thing was for real.

"When you are having a bad time, it's nice to have someone to commiserate with. David had always been the perfect companion for just these types of situations. He was cynical, disaffected, and funny. He had the ability to make any situation appear far worse than it was and make you laugh about it. There is comfort in that. But from the moment we stepped onto the mountain, he began acting weird.

"...David was focused and committed. He actually showed interest in learning how to do something he didn't know how to do for the first time in his life...The morning of the assault there were nerves all around as four boys and two giant mountaineers made their way in the dark before dawn to the first of the steep cliff faces we would navigate in our attempt to reach the summit...We were told that the youngest person to make the summit was sixteen. It wasn't clear if that was because nobody younger had attempted it or because they had tried and failed. If we made the summit, we would be the youngest group of climbers to accomplish this feat, and David would be the youngest individual to ever scale Mount Rainier. Quite an accomplishment, but still very uncertain.

"...We had been advised by Jim Whittaker to get into shape before out trek. He had suggested a regimen of running and some strengthening exercises. He didn't suggest that we stop smoking cigarettes. I'm sure he didn't feel there was a need given our age. David had stopped for a month.

"As they disappeared up the mountain, I felt a mixture of relief and longing not to be left behind – with a secret hope that they wouldn't make the summit, so I wouldn't be the only failure. I spent the nine hours of my isolation...looking off into the distance for a sign of the climbers return. It was a very long nine hours.

Behind Blue Eyes

As the sun was sinking and I was getting nervous about freezing to death, alone, eleven thousand feet up on Mount Rainier, I heard their voices. They had made the summit and were approaching me with the weary success of the conqueror.
My best friend in the world had become the youngest person to climb Mount Rainier – and I would never hear the end of it."

It seemed almost fitting that David's grandfather, Joseph Kennedy passed away just a few weeks prior to the close of the 1960s at the age of 81. There would be no talk of passing torches to the next generation however, as the new decade loomed.

Following Chappaquiddick, Joe represented the final link to the odyssey. In the space of a few years, those who had created and shaped the legacy – JPK, JFK and RFK, from whom David and the elder children were now standard bearers - had all departed. Just how the third wave of the family would mold and shape the legacy was yet to be determined. There was stormy weather waiting for the young Kennedys before they would emerge able to confidently deal with the mounting expectations.

If the past 18 months had proven traumatically dramatic for David, then the new decade would continue the trend. Without the guidance and leadership of his father, the rollercoaster that was his life, would career dangerously out of control at times. The events of June 1968 would reverberate through much of the disorientation David experienced in the new decade. He would himself dance with death – on more than one occasion. "From that day on, he was in a trance," Larry Newman asserted. "I never saw him normal a day the rest of his life."

Behind Blue Eyes

PART 2: DEEPER & DOWN
1970 - 1974

7. EVERY MAN FOR HIMSELF

At a time when David needed as much stability as possible, the start of the new decade saw his life undergo yet more flux and uncertainty. He switched from the Potomac School in McLean, Virginia to Middlesex Academy in Concord, Massachusetts largely to be closer to his cousin Chris Lawford. This was at a time when David felt increasingly alone within the family. Being closer to Chris would provide the emotional stability he felt he was not getting at Hickory Hill. Later, when reflecting on this time, David saw this as a critical period in his life. 1970 appeared to be the time that things started to go pear-shaped for David. "I remember it all clearly," he said many years later. "This was the point in my life when everything began to turn against me."

"When I went to boarding school at Middlesex, David was going to the Potomac School," Chris Lawford states, "and it was expected that he would continue there through high school. It didn't work out that way. David agreed to repeat ninth grade so we could be together at Middlesex. It surprised me that someone would like me enough to agree to repeat a whole year of school in order to be with me. It also made me a little uncomfortable - maybe because of the responsibility such a commitment implied.

"David was making a big commitment to our friendship," Lawford continued. "When it came time for me to do the same, I would bale. But this was way down the road – and still part of the great unknown. In this moment we were blissfully unaware and desperate for the feeling that there was someone in the world whose existence was enhanced by our life. We would reinforce our relationship by reminding each other that we were 'best friends to the bitter end.' David came up with our credo, and he loved it. It spoke to his need for an attachment to another and his need for permanence in that attachment. It was a lot to ask your buddy to stay back a grade, even if you were best friends, but that's what he did. We were in different grades, but it didn't matter – we were together."

Now leaderless since the death of RFK, many of the 2nd generation tried to fill the breech unsuccessfully, including JFK's old friend Lem Billings. "...Lem wanted to become a kind of surrogate dad to RFK's children, a role model," said Lawrence Quirk, who worked on JFK's 1946 congressional campaign. "But instead of guiding them and elevating them to his level, he ended up descending to theirs. His apartment became what in street vernacular is known as the 'corner candy store' – and LSD, hash, pot, coke and heroin den. Lem often plied the kids with drugs and became a rampant user himself. He was closest to Bobby jr, but he was also close to David as well as Chris Lawford...All three (became) addicted to drugs and hooked on booze."

Billings himself would lament the absence of the patriarch Joe Kennedy Sr. who died on November 18th, 1969. "If he could have lived as long and been in as good health as Mrs. Kennedy," he said, "it would have been so different for the next generation. He would have reached out and reeled them in. God knows they needed it."

The adults that were left to pick up the shattered pieces of the legacy were seemingly too deep in their own grief to fully help the 3rd generation.

Though David had never been particularly close to Ethel, the relationship with his mother had noticeably deteriorated since RFK's death.

"It was almost on general principle that she blamed me," David later commented. "Her idea was that it really didn't matter whether or not I had actually done anything. I would do it sooner or later so she might as well get heavy with me in advance."

The once happy Hickory Hill became something akin in David's words to "hell on earth." Things weren't as they appeared to outsiders.

"Those stories about what a big, happy family we had at Hickory Hill were all bullshit," David later told a friend. "Life at home was mayhem, a mess. My mother was always having screaming rages. The house looked like a shit-hole. She didn't know how to deal with so many kids. She didn't have the skills to raise 11 children. She didn't have the skills to run a house."

"Her talked a lot about his mom," a girlfriend from the mid 70s recalled for this author. "He thought she was pretty out there. He really wanted to be able to talk to her, but she wouldn't talk to him. She was pretty superficial in her discussions with him, or she'd browbeat him about not living up to his family's expectations. This was a real downer to him...His mom really could play a head game on him."

"What David was looking for was someone to really love him and be his friend," another pal said. "Ethel couldn't do it because she had too many kids and no patience."

While Ethel appeared to struggle to be emotionally available to David, she had a genuine concern about him. "We took him to a doctor and the doctor put him on some medication," Ethel told Noelle Bombardier. "One thing led to another and I think that's how he got addicted. But we were so worried about him; we just did what the doctors said. I think that's how it happened...I just don't know...I know there were sleeping pills because he couldn't sleep...I know that much."

David's relationship with his mother may have been challenging at this time, but he remained very close to his siblings. "David loved all his brothers and sisters," a girlfriend said to this author. "The younger ones were especially important to him. He didn't want them to know his dirt...He was close to one of his sisters – it might have been Courtney."

One memory that was told from these years spoke of the affection David and his siblings held for Hickory Hill in spite of the ensuing chaos.

"When they looked back at Hickory Hill, they saw those as blessed years," Laurence Leamer said. "Young Bobby in particular, felt that he and his brothers had had a little paradise in the woods and pastures around the house. He and his younger brothers had run free up and down the hills and meadows and streams of Pimmet Run, near Hickory Hill. Then one day the builders came and flattened the hills, covered the stream and felled the trees to build the Dolley Madison Highway, followed by homes and a strip mall. He and his brother David had taken some of the stacked pile of culvert pipes and sent them smashing down an embankment - their little act of sabotage."

The chaos extended to the hired help. Ethel went through cooks and maids at an alarming rate. Very few have fond memories. "It took five or six years before she realized I had a name," Said Mary De Grace, who did laundry for Ethel for seventeen years. "In the years following Bobby's death as the children grew up, I used to find pot in the laundry, in their pants pockets; especially with young David...You couldn't tell Ethel."

The help would also have to contend with the hormones of adolescent males. "The boys just tore them up and spat them out," recalled Richard Burke.

"The men in this family are all the same," said Theresa Fitzpatrick, who looked after Ted Kennedy's children. "They try to hit on anything in skirts that moves. Why Ethel's sons, Joe and David even tried to hit on me." When asked what she did about it, she smiled, "Told Joe to grow up and David I slapped the daylights out of – how's that?"

Despite the ensuing chaos, there were always visitors staying over. "The RFKs' all slept with these big noisy fans in the windows of their bedrooms," Chris Lawford explained. "I think it must have been a Skakel thing because no other Kennedys do it. This went on year-round. No matter how cold it got, the windows were open and the fans were on. I slept over at the RFKs' so much it became a habit with me too, which continues to this day. One of those nights at Hickory Hill I woke to find that the fan had shorted out and set the window drapes on fire. I yelled to David, who was curled up under a pile of comforters that the room was on fire. It always took David a while to wake up. This time was no different. He lifted his head up from the pile of blankets, he noticed the fire racing up the window treatments, looked at me and said, "Have a little consideration and put it out man, I'm trying to sleep."

Richard Burke, an aide to Teddy for ten years, saw David on many occasions. Although he was only two years older, something disturbed him.

"I was troubled by Bobby and David, who were close to my age," he said. "Both seemed out of control. David, especially, impressed me as being only vaguely associated with reality, and he often bore the brunt of his mother's distress...

"I mentioned my concerns to the Senator, who shared them," Burke furthered. "He knew they needed fatherly guidance, a strong hand to compliment Ethel's own...but he had his own family and career to manage, and handling eleven of his brother's children was too much for any man, even a Kennedy...He knew there was going to be trouble regardless of what he did. It was like waiting for a storm to blow in; there was nothing to do but take cover."

With the spotlight on the new generation of Kennedys, most still only teenagers, it came as no surprise as many struggled with the magnitude of the burden they now shouldered.

"From an early age our purpose was to become more Kennedy," Chris Lawford wrote. "More brave, more reckless, more teeth, more charisma, better sailors, better football players, better with the ladies. This is what we were looking for – what we would have liked to recreate – but we never had a snowball's chance in hell of doing it. The premature deaths of Jack and Bobby Kennedy elevated them to mythic proportions. Their greatness was undiminished, their human failings forgotten. They were our benchmarks, which on a deep unspoken level we knew we would never reach. I think David knew this before any of us. It's what fueled his sardonic side."

David's eldest brother, and oldest male of the third generation of Kennedys, Joseph II shouldered the heaviest burden of expectation. "We felt a real pressure to be worthy of the name Kennedy." Joe said. "There was always so much emphasis on being of service. 'Make your life count' was something we heard a lot. Even if someone wasn't preaching it to us in the moment, all you had to do was think about the family's history and how important Jack and Bobby and even Ted had been to America to feel sort of overwhelmed by it. So, as a kid, yes, I think the best way to put it is that we were overwhelmed by it all and it could be said we acted out because of it."

"...Nobody had the time or inclination to give us the attention we needed to move down a road of our own choosing," Lawford concluded. "So we created our own secret life. A life we had some control over, we thought. It was as if we knew it was all a horrible joke and we acted out in our outrageousness to let them know we knew."

"We were often reminded that this country has been very good to the Kennedys and that we owed it some kind of reciprocal debt in return," Bobby Kennedy Jr stated. "That the money was just not all ours and the privilege and the power was not just ours to do what we wanted with, that we had to use it in some way to serve others, otherwise we would be wasting what we'd been given. I remember one time when my father returned from Appalachia where he found three families living in a one-room shack and the kids were going to bed hungry. And he came back home just in time for dinner and over the meal he said to us, 'You know, you're lucky to be eating all this food in this wonderful house where you have your own rooms to sleep in, and I hope and pray that when you guys grow up you'll be able to do something to help people.' We clearly heard Saint Luke's admonition that from those who have been given much, much shall be expected. Was it pressure? Yes...Our mother did the best she could, but in her defense there was pretty much no way to handle us. We were pretty bad."

David's growing awareness of his own uniqueness within the family, started to manifest as a distancing from the illusions that the previous generations of Kennedys held so dear. He appeared to be yearning for what was true and solid among the myths so as to build something stable for himself amidst the ruins of Camelot.

"David did seem to cling onto the idealism of his dad," one close friend told this author in 2009, "perhaps because that is the only thing that made any sense. It at least, was real. The love David shared with his family cannot be discounted though.

"But the way I saw David," the woman continued, "was as a very upright, honest individual; he didn't try to be something he was not. He was the real McCoy – or Kennedy – and if nothing else in life made any sense, I always knew I had a friend in David. Unfortunately for him as well as his family, that quality did not seem to fit in with the Camelot myth. I heard David call it that numerous times. He seemed to be disenchanted with his family and the establishment in general."

"You'd find him lost in a book or magazine in the far corner of some store," Chris Lawford remembers, "his hair a mess flying in a hundred different directions, the shirttails of his Brooks Brothers button-down shirt hanging out, and the sleeves messily rolled to different lengths on his skinny arms. He would be completely oblivious to the fact that you might have been looking for him for the last hour or so and not apologetic in the slightest."

It was no surprise, considering the growing emotional estrangement and isolation, that David chose to spend as little time at home as possible. In the summer of 1970, the now 15-year-old David hitchhiked to New York City with Cousin Chris Lawford. It was here that the two teenagers used heroin for the first time. They arrived in the big apple dirty and disheveled. There was also the problem of being broke. To make themselves more financially solvent, they panhandled at Grand Central Station for a few hours every morning.

"It was great just being ordinary people and not Kennedys," David later said. "Also, it wasn't bad money. At one point when were making the equivalent of about forty dollars an hour."

Patricia Lawford, David's aunt and mother of Chris had left the US with her daughters for Paris, leaving vacant her apartment on the corner of Eighth Street and Fifth Avenue. David and Chris moved in.

"She had vacated her apartment...leaving only the rugs and a kitchen full of canned food and broken utensils," Chris recalled in his autobiography. "My cousin David and I had sleeping bags, which were all we needed to take up residence. We hung out in Central Park at a place called Dope Hill where the elite of the drug culture congregated. Heroin was four dollars a bag and you could get high on three bags. That wasn't a lot of money, but we were high school kids on hiatus with very little cash.

Behind Blue Eyes

"David and I would head down to the (family) office, and after unsuccessfully trying to convince the family accountant Gertrude Ball to give us an advance on monies we were supposed to get at twenty-one, we would head down to Grand Central for three hours of panhandling. We had a notion that we were living some kind of bohemian, hippy lifestyle, begging for quarters in our bare feet and then running out to our commune of junkies in Central Park. We were free from any authority and it felt good. We had the illusion that we were living our own life. We had our own money, a crash pad, and some new friends."

"One day we decided to have a party. It was our intention to invite every girl we could find in and around Dope Hill. We figured if we invited fifty good-looking girls and a few guys the odds that we might get lucky would be heavily in our favor. On the day, we spread out and invited fifty of the hottest young hippie chicks we could find in Central Park. We bought some soda and beer and waited for the influx of willing beauty that was sure to descend on 990 Fifth Avenue that evening.

"...I was more nervous than David. It was my mother's apartment and her doormen, after all. My ass is on the line if she found out. David once again demonstrated contempt for my cries of alarm."

DAVID: Why are you getting so uptight?
CHRIS: Have you taken a look at these people, man?
DAVID: What about them? You invited them.
CHRIS: WE invite them. And we didn't invite them. We invited the girls.
DAVID: The girls came. Did you see the one with long brown hair and the enormous breasts?
CHRIS: She's beautiful.
DAVID: She's mine. I saw her first.
CHRIS: Fuck you. I saw her first.
DAVID: Don't be an asshole. I saw her first.

"There was no sense in arguing. Even if David was wrong he would argue until he wore you down and you gave him what he wanted.
"CHRIS: Whatever man. Just help me get all these junkies out of my mom's apartment."

A later girlfriend told of the bond between the two Kennedy cousins. "David and Chris were really close," she told this author, "but they both wanted Bobby's approval more than anything...even more than Joe's. Chris would blow David off if Bobby was around. I think they both used each other as whipping boys so Bobby would acknowledge them positively.

"David and Chris were really brothers under the skin," the girlfriend thought, "but if David had a chance he'd give Chris a hard time...He always called Chris the pretty boy, movie star. I never thought Chris was half as handsome as David. David was a golden guy with those wonderful blue eyes, straw blond hair and a smile that would break your heart. He totally captured mine, and I thought he hung the moon. I would of and did do anything I could for him."

Arriving back at Hyannis Port a week after his NYC jaunt, Ethel showed no signs of knowing that David was gone. He regularly slept in the in the hedges behind the house, as did Bobby jr who also resorted to stealing food from nearby houses. The Camelot Express had clearly derailed.

At the end of the school year in June '71, Ethel told David that he was being sent to the Blackfoot Reservation in Montana. "My father had been involved with the Indians," David observed. "She was obviously hoping that having an experience with the downtrodden would awaken my hereditary social conscience."

Tribal elders named him Yellow Dove for his fair appearance and his father's message of peace. He attended tribal functions and ceremonial occasions. But he was far more interested in the marijuana field he and a friend discovered.

They were staying with a native-American couple who were shocked to discover David preparing the pot in their humble abode. The woman, David said, "Was standing there looking at me with this strange expression on her face as if to say, 'What is the son of Robert Kennedy doing making marijuana tea in my kitchen?'"

Back at Middlesex that autumn, David and Chris were increasingly under the allegiance of Bobby Jr who was starting to find his feet. "...The younger Kennedys, brothers and cousins, would come up to Cambridge and just wander around forlornly if Bobby wasn't there to lead them," Joey Brode remembered.

Now that he was on the threshold of manhood, the dares that his brothers taunted him with would have a darker edge to them. David, knowing that courage was his father's most admired personal trait, would risk life and limb in order to prove himself. Perhaps confusing recklessness with bravery, he would always accept his siblings' dares, feeling that this was his only way to shine.

"He was highly influenced by Joe and especially Bobby," a girlfriend said of David. "If Bobby did it, David had to do it better and make it a bit harder or more challenging."

At 17, David, like others in his immediate group, had a rapidly growing reputation for derring-do. He would maintain his thirst for risky behavior for the rest of his life. Andy Karsch recalled an instance where a number of youths, David included, were throwing snowballs at Harvard Square. When one hit a car, it abruptly pulled up and a large man emerged and approached them.

"He was yelling about our irresponsibility," Karsch said. "And we were sort of retreating as he walked toward us. All of a sudden David, all 120 pounds (55 kg) of him, steps up and punches this guy right in the face. The rest of us were too petrified to run. David looked over at Bobby with this dumb grin as if to say: 'There, are you proud of me now? This huge guy stands there for a minute with an absolutely dumbfounded look on his face, then just shakes his head in disbelief and gets back in the car and drives off."

His risky behavior extended to 'soft' drugs, now a regular habit. In addition to frequent marijuana use, he'd drop acid once a week with his morning coffee. He was also fast developing a taste for liquor, although his problems here would still be a several years down the road.

Distinct differences were emerging in the characters of David's two eldest brothers as they entered their 20s. While David admired Joe, it was Bobby to whom he gravitated and sought approval. "The difference between Joe and Bobby is substantial," commented one Kennedy insider in a 1977 interview.

"While Joe would make an excellent public servant, he doesn't have the intellect or the temperament that Bobby has. Joe has quite a temper along with his good looks. I guess the older children always have more problems than the younger ones. But Bobby is the one to watch. He is bright as a star, a damn good speaker and writer, and he is definitely going places."

Bobby for his part was more diplomatic about his rising star. "There are a lot of us," Bobby told a journalist in 1978. "I have a lot of brother and sisters around and other relatives — there are Lawfords and Shrivers and Smiths and some of them will undoubtedly go into politics. My brother Joe ran my uncle's campaign from top to bottom and he got us working on it. Joe stepped into my father's shoes and we all look up to him."

Following in Bobby's footsteps extended to David's schooling too, where he would be suspended like his elder brother. In the spring of '72 a pound of marijuana that he had hidden his suitcase (sold to him by Bobby), was stolen. Bobby showed up in drug-dealer mode and put the fear of God into the thief. David said he didn't know the dealer by name but Bobby was recognized.

The spirited high jinks were never far away from Hickory Hill either. "Joe was David's favorite target," Chris Lawford observed. "I don't remember many football games that didn't end with Joe getting into a fight with somebody. Joe was a bull on the football field. He was a big, bruising, snorting presence; and if nobody waved a red cape in front of him he was more or less controlled. But it was only a matter of time before somebody waved the cape – and it was usually David.

"We all knew how to make Joe crazy," Lawford furthered. "It wasn't hard. All you had to do was question a call or disagree with a play he called, and all hell would break loose. It was a very dangerous thing to do, and most of us didn't have the guts for it. But David couldn't wait. It was like a game to him. He'd show little pieces of red, and Joe's frustration and anger would build until that moment when David let the red cape fly.

DAVID: Joe, why don't you let someone else call a play?

Behind Blue Eyes

JOE: Because I'm quarterback.
DAVID: Maybe it's time you let someone else be quarterback, Joe.
JOE: I'm the quarterback!!
DAVID: It doesn't seem fair, Joe.
JOE: It's fair because I say it's fair!!
DAVID: You don't have to get mad, Joe.
JOE: All right, David, that does it!!

"Joe would explode and chase David all over the field. Joe would almost catch him and David would slide or duck, and Joe would come up empty. David would laugh and admonish Joe to calm down. Joe would just get angrier and angrier until he would give up and storm off threatening to never play football again. It was like watching Roadrunner torture Wyley Coyote."

The Robert F. Kennedy Memorial Foundation hosted an annual charity pet show on the grounds of Hickory Hill at the start of each summer. Richard Burke was one that was actively involved for the 1972 event.

"I was upstairs at Hickory Hill late one morning, attending to my duties, when Bobby and David appeared," Burke said. "They were attired only in white jockey shorts, looking as if they had just crawled out of bed, with glassy eyes and dazed expressions. Their shoulder-length hair, Bobby's brown and curly; David's blond and nearly straight, was decidedly bedraggled. They grunted a 'good morning.' Probably not sure what time of day it was."

"...I turned my attention to a garden out back," Burke continued. "I grabbed a hoe and began poking at a scruffy-looking plot in a corner of the yard that appeared to be overgrown with a ragged-leafed weed. Suddenly I heard a voice scream at my back, 'Rick, Rick, stop!'

I turned to see David, now fully alert and clearly worried, still clad only in shorts, running toward me. 'What?' I asked.
'Just leave that alone.' He said. 'Don't touch it.'
'Why? It looks messy.'

'Don't worry,' he advised me. 'We're putting a fence around it. You could do us a favor. Put a fence around it. But just don't touch it.'
'Okay, fine.'
David said, 'Great, Rick. Thanks.' Then he disappeared back inside the house.

...If (Ethel) didn't see a problem (with growing pot), I certainly wasn't going to raise it."

"The devastating truth is that most of Ethel's sons would become alcoholics or drug addicts," Laurence Leamer observed. "They may well have had a gene that increased their propensity for such problems, but that hardly accounts for this plague. Their home became a virtual machine for creating addiction, the type of environment written about in any number of psychological textbooks and spoken of with deep, painful truth by addicts in AA meetings."

Later in the summer, Ethel once again sought a socially redeeming trip for David. She sent him and Chris Lawford to work in the lettuce fields of La Paz, California with Cesar Chavez. "Your father felt he was one of the most moral men he'd ever met," Ethel told David. "Maybe he'll do you some good."

During their month-long stay, he and Chris picked up the garbage left from the farm workers for 2 dollars an hour. "It was pretty much a disaster from the start," Lawford recalled. "We showed up smoking Marlboro cigarettes and drinking Coors beer – both of which were being boycotted by the UFW for unfair labor practices. The good people at the UFW thought we were coming out to work. We thought we were gonna hang out and rub shoulders with some frontline activists. We were more interested in our tans than in the nitty-gritty of social change. We spent our days assigned to the garbage collection detail, sneaking off when we could for an hour of sunbathing. Our nights were spent in the bunkhouse drinking beer, doing speed, staying up all night arguing about who was smarter, and fantasizing about all the fun we were gonna have when we got the hell out of La Paz. It was clear that we were not yet ready to pick up the mantle."

The two seventeen-year-olds decided to visit Chris' father Peter at his Malibu home. "I knocked on the door and there's Peter Lawford," David said. "I hadn't seen him in years. The first thing he does after saying hello was offer me a pipe full of hash."

"Bobby Jr and David were perpetually high on something," Richard Burke said. "Usually pot...You'd go into the house in the morning and the place would reek of pot. Ethel didn't have a clue; she didn't know what it was."

8. PAM

Laurence Leamer writes: "He was a handsome young man with deep set eyes that seemed to advertise his vulnerability. His neediness and candor appealed to many women though his temper flared at the most inopportune of times. David sought to tear away the Kennedy nameplate from in front of his life...He had no sense of his real fundamental human value and drugs were a way to obliterate that reality."

"David was actually much better looking than most of his photos show," said a girlfriend to this author. "He was by far the best looking of all the Kennedy males, and in my opinion that included JFK Jr, but I was biased...He really had a sparkle and charisma that came out when you knew him."

But it was the getting to know him that was the challenge. Many suggest that he remained very guarded. "He didn't let anyone get close to him," Larry Newman said. "He went with a number of girls, one after the other. He had a bravado about him. A lot of people took it for arrogance, but it was just to cover up what he was feeling."

Pam Kelley was one girl that David allowed into his inner world. She was 19, a year older than David, attractive with long blond hair and rimless glasses. She and David hooked up in June 1973, just before Ethel sent David away again for another summer trip. She told him that she too was having problems with her parents and asked if she and a girlfriend could join him. The Kelley family had been friends with the Kennedys for years, and while Pam had known his older siblings well, she told David that she couldn't remember seeing him around much.

"I've been around," he replied. "But I haven't been around with the rest of the family. I've been more by myself. That's just the way it is."

"He didn't have the hardness or the physicality of the rest of them; David was always the soft one," she said.

Their road trip lasted 6 weeks, which included a month at Caribou Ranch, outside of Boulder, Colorado, where Ethel had lined up a job for David doing manual labor. Pam and David got together after David struck out with Pam's girlfriend who returned home shortly after. "I told him I'd had a terrible year," she recalls, "and that I'd been feeling nobody loved me. He smiled that wounded, angelic smile of his and said that he'd been going through the same thing. We sort of decided to love each other."

Ethel soon found out about their tryst. "She went around complaining how the Kelley girls were always seducing her boys," Pam commented. "That was a laugh."

Not being able to stay at the ranch together anymore, Pam slept in the Chevy Impala that David had driven across the country. By day, she watched David shovel chicken manure. When he finished work, they would head into boulder for beers and games of pool.

On their way home in early August, they picked up a hitchhiker. Dropping him off at St. Louis, the young man said they should pop into his parents place in New Orleans. "This boy had called ahead and when we showed up his mother had everything ready," Pam said. "The only thing was that she had arranged to put us in two different bedrooms. David asked if we could sleep together and she said yes. It was a wonderful week we spent there. They had a swimming pool, wine for dinner every evening. She gave us dimes to ride the trolley downtown."

David and Pam arrived back at Hyannis Port on Saturday, August 11. Pam dropped off her stuff at her family's house and then she and David went onto Ethel's. They stayed in a Playhouse in the backyard. "It was a Saturday night," Pam remembered. "We slept in this tiny miniature bed and the next morning David got up and said, 'Uh-oh, I've got to go to eleven o'clock mass.' I said, 'What am I supposed to do, stay in this two-by-two house and wait? No way. I'll sneak out and meet you someplace for lunch.' David panicked and said for me to sit tight because his mother would go into a rage if she knew I was with him. Then he left. I started my period that night, the little white room of the Playhouse was half red - the sheets, the mattress, and the rest of the little miniature bed. I just rolled everything into one bloody pile and bolted. I was scared of Ethel, who was always hysterical even when she wasn't mad. I thought that if I was caught she'd hang me from the Compound flagpole."

She met up with David later that day, who had received a call from his brother Joe inviting him to a barbeque with his friends at Nantucket. "David was ecstatic," Pam recalled. "Here, finally, someone in the family was taking notice of him."

David and Pam spent Sunday sailing with Joe and that night had a barbeque on the beach. Next morning they went for a swim before they caught the ferry back. Joe borrowed a friend's jeep to drive them all to the jetty.

David said that Joe tried to give him the attention that he needed but was too distracted by his own issues. "Joe had problems of his own and couldn't keep his mind on me for more than a few minutes at a time. It had reached that point in our family where it was every man for himself."

"He was doing his Super-Kennedy act," David said of his brother on the afternoon of August 13th, 1973. "There was all this crazy energy. I suppose Teddy was that way before Chappaquiddick." Pam Kelley describes what happened next on that Monday afternoon: "We were all sort of standing up in the jeep. Joe was cutting through the woods, spinning the jeep in circles. We were all yelling and laughing and acting crazy. There was a rest area on the other side of the highway and Joe started to cross over to it. He didn't see this station wagon heading toward us until the last minute. Joe swerved and we hit a ditch with our tires on the right side, breaking the jeep's axle and flipping us. We held on to the roll bar for a couple of flips and then had to let go. Me and David were right together…in the air. I remember tumbling and seeing David's face. I hit the ground. When I tried to get up, nothing happened."

Driver of the oncoming car, Merrill Lindsay said he was lucky not to among the injured. "I was confronted with a jeep full of people heading toward me on my side of the road," he said. Lindsay slammed on the brakes, and the Kennedy vehicle "missed me by a hair. As the jeep was passing me, I saw people flying out of it," he said.

Passer-by Luke Gruber said he saw the open-air vehicle fail to make the curve and flip over. "One girl was thrown 25 or 30 feet," Gruber said. "Two were on their feet right away. One was sitting there and talking, but he apparently couldn't get up. That must have been David Kennedy, but we didn't know who they were until later."

The accident occurred as the seven were heading from Siasconset on the eastern end of Nantucket to the other side of the island. All were dressed in beach wear. Those involved in the accident were flown by plane to Cape Cod Hospital in Hyannis except for one girl, who was treated at Nantucket Hospital and released. The women who were uninjured were Patricia Powers, 22, of Spring Lake, N.J., her sister Kimberly Kelley Powers, 17, and Francesca Dennis, 18, of Centerville, Mass.

Later that afternoon in the lobby of the hospital, family members had started to arrive. Ethel, highly agitated, stopped a nurse walking by. "I demand to see my sons."

"Why are you standing there looking at me?" Jean Smith asked when the nurse glanced across to her. "We've been standing out here for an hour and no one has said a single word to us about anything."

When told the doctor would be available soon to give them an update, Ethel, exhaustedly collapsed into a chair.

"As you can see, Mrs. Kennedy is very upset," Jean stated. To Rose's assistant, Barbara Gibson, she said, "Call my husband (Stephen Smith) and ask him to meet us here as soon as he can get here. Tell him that David and Joe have been in a car accident and we need him here."

As Gibson went to find a phone, she heard Ethel tell Jean, "I don't know what these kids have done now. And I'm afraid to find out."

After another hour-and-a-quarter, following Steve Smith's arrival at the hospital, a doctor emerged with young Joe, looking pale and shaken.

"Thank God," Ethel exclaimed hugging her son. She then studied his face and smacked him on the shoulder. "Where's David? And what happened? You tell me this instant what happened?"

"It's my fault," Joe replied. "David's here because of me, Mom. It's because of me...I guess I was driving too fast, and on the way back in the jeep, it somehow overturned and everyone sort of spilled out of it."

"What do you mean you guess you were driving too fast?" Ethel demanded.

"Okay, I was driving too fast, Mom, and now everyone's hurt except me. I don't know what else to say."

"Ethel broke down when she heard about that accident," Leah Mason recalled. "She was inconsolable. 'My own boys are responsible for this,' she later said, 'which makes me responsible...'"

A local newspaper duly reported the accident the following day:

HYANNIS, (UPI) David Kennedy, 18, the son of the late Sen. Robert Kennedy, suffered a sprained back in a car accident Monday. Five young women were in the jeep-like vehicle, driven by David's brother Joseph P. Kennedy III, 21, when it failed to make a curve and overturned. Joseph Kennedy escaped injury, but one of the .five girls was hospitalized in serious condition.

Three of the other girls were treated and released at Cape Cod Hospital in Hyannis, and one remained hospitalized, but she was listed in good condition.

Nantucket police charged Joseph Kennedy with "driving negligently so that the lives and safety of the public might have been endangered." He was ordered to appear at a court hearing next week. All except Joseph Kennedy were thrown from the vehicle before it landed upside down in brush on Nantucket Island.

David was admitted to Cape Cod Hospital where he was reported in satisfactory condition. Pamela Kelley, 19, of Centerville, Mass., the most seriously injured underwent surgery Monday night for an apparent spinal injury and was listed in serious condition. Mary Schlaff, 22, of Grosse Pointe, Michigan, also was admitted to the hospital, where she was listed in good condition with a possible pelvic fracture. A spokesman at Cape Cod Hospital reported that David was "resting comfortably" overnight.

Pam Kelley was operated on for more than three hours at the hospital. Dr. William R. Torgerson and Dr. Charles A. Fager, both neurosurgeons of the Lahey Clinic Foundation in Boston, helped perform the operation. Her prognosis was grim. Her family would wait anxiously for good news. Pam's mom, Margaret said to the waiting media, "It's too early to say how she will be. We won't know for two weeks." It soon became apparent the seriousness of Pam's injury. She would be paralyzed from the chest down.

David was less severely injured than Pam but suffered considerable pain with a badly sprained back. He was in a traction device and unable to move. He read Hunter Thompson's Fear and Loathing: On the Campaign Trail 1972 with the aid of prismatic glasses.

When Ethel and the others were finally allowed to see David, she was shocked at his condition. He was lying there just staring up at the ceiling. Fearing serious injury, she quickly went to his bedside, unable to hide her concern. "Whatever happened, it doesn't matter." Ethel told David. "As long as you're okay." As David glanced across to his mother, a single tear trickled down his cheek. "I'm sorry mom."

In the process of treating David's pain, the doctors unwittingly awoke a sleeping giant. "The first time he felt time he felt good after his father died was in the hospital after the accident when they gave him morphine," a Harvard friend said.

"It felt great, just great," David remembered. "I'd drift off to sleep and wake up and figure it was eight hours later and time for my next shot. Then I'd look at my watch and realize that it had only been an hour and a half. I'd start yelling in agony to get them to hurry up."

"Taking morphine," David furthered, "that's when I really felt for the first time that things were okay in my life. The morphine man, it was the thing that made me forget how miserable I had been since Dad died. It was the thing that made me forget my pain."

However distraught she may have been privately, in public, as always, her façade never crumbled. Pam recalls Ethel cheerily breezing into her hospital room with other members of the family with cookies and laughter. The artificialness of it all was too much for David.

"She just can't be real, or she'll fall apart," David angrily told Pam. "And she can't fall apart because she's Ethel Kennedy and Ethel Kennedy can never fall apart. It's a vicious cycle."

When David found out that his family was discussing a possible million dollar settlement with the Kelley's, he became furious. He was still not supposed to get out of bed, but did so rather woodenly, and walked into Pam's room.

"That fucking bitch friend of yours, he yelled. "You wouldn't believe the shit she's been telling me...!"

Pam was amazed that David had been left in the dark, and told him that it was true.

As David improved, and eventually left the hospital, some 8 days after the accident, he used his time to come and visit Pam. "He'd come and see me and then tell the doctors that the pain in his back was intense and that they had to readmit him," Pam said.

"We would spend long hours together at the hospital just rapping," Pam recalled. "He was very concerned about me and very upset when a lot of people would be around for any period of time. We had a very strong bond. Both of us had problems and we talked and talked about them. He was trying to come out from the shadow of his older brothers and he was trying to figure out how he should move ahead in his life. He was so very sensitive. The accident just made him more so."

"This was the beginning of the end for David," Chris Lawford thought. "I don't think he was ever the same after the accident. Things would go from bad to very bad to worse in a very short time. The years after the accident were the worst years, by far."

Despite Joe's culpability for the accident that devastated several lives, David tried to reassure his big brother about the legal ramifications. "Uncle Teddy didn't go to jail after Chappaquiddick," David told Joe on the day on his sentencing, "and that was a lot worse than this. So I don't think you have to worry too much."

"I sure hope you're right," Joe anxiously responded.

Joe indeed avoided jail time, charged with negligent driving and fined what many thought to be a paltry $100. Judge C. George Anastos, had ironically been a Harvard law school classmate of Joe's namesake and Uncle in the 1930s. The event was a life altering moment. For his part, Joe started to build a solid, respectable life as pre-determined for him by the family. His reckless youth had come at a heavy price for his passengers however.

Tensions soon arose in David and Pam's relationship from the frustrations of her permanent paralysis. He would occasionally call and be argumentative.

"It reached the point where I'd just have to say, 'Look, I'm sorry David. I know what your needs are but I've just got to hang up now,'" Pam said. "A few minutes later the phone would ring and I'd hear this enraged voice scream, 'You're an asshole!' and then he'd slam the receiver down."

They broke up that autumn. "You finally find someone to love," David said of Pam, "and you lose her. It's the shits."

9. NASHVILLE THEN HARVARD

David was back at Middlesex Academy that autumn of '73 to start his final year of high school. He began chasing the high he felt when the doctors administered morphine in the hospital a few weeks earlier. Though he was convinced that he could take it or leave it, David said he was "swallowing Percodans and shooting heroin," all through his senior year.

"With heroin you don't feel any pain," David stated. "You could lose your girlfriend, your father, everything on the same day – and you wouldn't feel a thing...Heroin is that good."

His sister Kathleen became the first of the third generation to marry when in the autumn of 1973 she tied the knot with David Townsend. Again highlighting how closely good and bad fortune walked with the Kennedys, it was the same day Teddy Jr had a cancerous leg removed. Ted Sr rushed to the church to give away the young bride.

David had always admired his big sister's stability and common sense and had even hoped to stay with her and her new husband.

"David really loved his family," said a girlfriend to this author. "He had a complicated relationship with his older brothers and his mom, but the younger ones and the girls were very loving. He worried about how he came off to them. He told me once that he wished he could have gone out to Sante Fe and stayed with Kathleen and her husband David right after they were married. He said she was very even-keeled and a good influence on him. He felt that it would have been a safe place for him."

While his eldest contemporaries had a major impact during his developing adolescent and early adult years, his father remained the biggest inspiration in his life.

"His dad was a big influence on what as a teen David was seeking out," a girlfriend from this time period recalled for this author. "He was still looking for a way to fill that void as much as his dad had done when (JFK) was killed, if that makes sense. We talked a lot about that kind of stuff. We both had lost parents and delved into that sorrow with each other.

"When we first met I didn't know he was a Kennedy," the woman furthered. "That only came out later as we continued to share about dealing with our lives without the central parent.

"He really wanted to make his dad proud of him in spite of the fact he had died," she went on. "He really felt the weight of his dad's death strongly. He really loved him, and felt his dad understood him.

"He planned on us going to DC to his dad's grave," the girlfriend remembered. "He said we could go near our birthdays. He said he had to go as a command performance right before those dates for the anniversary of his dad's death, but he wanted us to go as normal people. He wanted to grieve as anonymously as he could. He said I could mourn my mom there too."

One of the ways David's mother Ethel thought might help him find his feet was by connecting him to some of his dad's old friends.

"You got the feeling," said a friend of David's, "that Ethel kept sending him around to all of the old family friends in hopes that one night somebody would sit down and have the talk with him that would make the difference."

One RFK friend she thought might make a difference was John Seigenthaler. He had worked as Bobby's assistant in the justice department and was working in a field that interested David: journalism. He was a talented editor (of the Nashville Tennessean), devoted to RFK, and a protector of his legacy. In April 1974, David was welcomed onboard – but no favors were given or expected.

"I told the staff not to do him any special favors just because I knew the family," Seigenthaler recalled. "He didn't need them. He was bright as he could be, and before the summer was over he had gone beyond what he was hired for and gotten no less than eight stories in the paper. He was pretty good."

David spent his 4 months with the newspaper productively: developing his considerable writing skills, making several new contacts and generally thriving in an atmosphere of independence from the family. Nashville also appealed because of his father's victory over arch nemesis Jimmy Hoffa several years before. In July he relocated to the paper's Washington bureau for 3 weeks. It appeared he'd found his vocational path.

"David could have been an outstanding journalist," Seigenthaler recalled fondly. "He had an inquisitive mind and was not afraid of hard work. He learned quickly and had a remarkable and rare talent for writing a simple, declarative sentence."

Not so positive was his physical appearance. He arrived at the Tennessean capital gaunt and sickly looking. "David was the skinniest little kid, a mass of shirttails hanging out," John Warnecke, son of the architect who designed JFK's grave and a campaign worker for RFK in 1968, said. "He was shooting smack; that was clear to anyone who knew drugs. I had the only hot tub in Nashville...I invited him over. He came and took off his jacket and these little popper syringes and packets of white stuff would fall out..."

Managing editor of the Tennessean, Wayne Whitt said that the staff remained in the dark about his drug use. "If he had a drug problem, we were not aware of it," Whitt commented. "But he didn't look good the whole time he was here. He never looked real healthy. He was real frail looking."

One of his first duties was not associated with the paper, but with his family. In 1974, Vanderbilt University in Nashville hosted the inaugural State Special Olympics, a concept founded by David's Aunt Eunice Shriver – a champion for the handicapped. Since the event was hosted by the Joseph P. Kennedy Foundation, it was appropriate that David was invited to attend. David's other Aunt, Jean Kennedy-Smith, handed out the awards, while David led the young charges through their motto: "Let me win, but if I cannot win, let me be brave in the attempt."

At the Tennessean, he was initially hired as a copy boy, but after two weeks persuaded Whitt that he should be allowed to contribute stories. Whitt said he wasn't alone in saying David showed great promise as a writer. Staff regarded his best piece to be the lead story he wrote on locusts. "With orange eyes protruding from their short wide heads," David wrote, "millions of insects will fill the air over a third of Tennessee in the coming weeks with an incessant drumming noise."

David initially boarded with the Seigenthalers, staying up late most nights drinking beer and reminiscing about his dad. Seigenthaler remembered one such time at his house when he asked David if he could remember visiting Nashville before – he said he couldn't. A photo album was produced for David's perusal. They were taken in 1968 when Bobby had made a speech at Vanderbilt University on the campaign trail.

He appeared transfixed on the forgotten memories. "It was as if he were trying to get a fix on a valuable piece of history that he had forgotten," John Seigenthaler later recalled. "David looked at himself in those pictures like they were a strange sort of mirror," Seigenthaler continued. "He looked at them a half-dozen times at least, mesmerized by them, and he kept asking me questions. There was a tremendous desire to know his father, to really know him. There was also a tremendous desire to know the person he himself had been in those pictures and was no longer."

Seigenthaler recalls another time when his mother had invited them over for lunch one Sunday. The elder Seigenthaler mentioned a book with a quote that she wanted to share with her guests, but couldn't locate the book. She spoke out loud for Saint Anthony's help – the finder of lost articles. David told his elderly companion that Anthony was his patron saint and that he was named after him. When the book was later discovered, she firmly believed David had played a role in locating the book. David laughingly took credit for it.

Although Seigenthaler denies seeing any signs of drug abuse, it appears he was still using clandestinely during his Nashville period – though how frequently cannot be stated accurately.

"He was doing heroin when I met him," his main girlfriend at this time, Claire told this author in 2009, "but he wasn't what I thought of as a druggie. He seemed to handle it well. I don't know if that was true, or just me wanting to believe it was. He was so out of the realm of the ordinary for me.

"He seemed to find the seedier parts of Nashville," Claire concluded. "He was just then dabbling in heavier drugs. He thought he could stop when he wanted to."

One female friend says that "he was the most decadent person I had ever seen. He used that quality to his advantage with women, who felt that they could be the ones to save him. He was very interested in writing and history, but he was already heavy into drugs then. Every time I saw him he was stoned on marijuana."

"We'd talk and he'd say how the family treated him so bad," John Warnecke said. "His brothers were doing everything he was doing and he was the one taking the heat from Ethel. It became clear that he thought of himself and in fact was what they call in family therapy 'the designated sick one,' the one whose sickness allows everyone else to feel healthy by comparison."

"I knew David from the early-mid seventies until he passed," Claire recalls of the man who had a special impact on her life. "I loved him very much. He was an important part of my formation as an adult. It's still very difficult for me to talk about him...

"I was a pretty typical girl for David," Claire said of herself. "I am a hazel-eyed, brunette with a good build. I'm about 5'5". He always kidded me that I caught his eye because I was his 'type'. You have to remember that we were really young when we met. I think he just liked my chest. I was, and have always been curvy, but I'm not heavy. He said that I had a Marilyn Monroe build. I didn't know (about his affinity with her) back then. I just thought he thought I was nicely built. He used to pick on me about being a Belle Meade Belle. He said that was a southern version of a Philadelphia Mainliner.

"We actually met at mass," Claire says of her initial meeting with David. "My brother had dropped me off, and was skipping mass. David slid in my row. Remember, I didn't know who he was, so he was just this really cute guy at mass. When he slid in the pew I thought he was so cute. He had killer eyes and a bit of shameful look where he was late. I remember he looked at me and shrugged his shoulders and gave me that amazing smile. I was instantly in 'love' as most young girls would have been of a cute new guy showing up in their parish.

"After mass, I was hanging around where my brother was late," Claire continued. "He was just kind of waiting too and we started talking. He asked me where my folks were, why I was alone in mass; most people sat with families then. I told him my mom was dead. We talked a bit more and he got my number. After he went back to school he'd still call on occasion until he passed.

"David didn't forget people," Claire stated. "I might not hear from him for months and then would call. He seemed to stay in touch with ex's. At that time in his life, he said he wasn't going to mass much unless it was mandatory. He told me he had woken up and felt he needed to be in mass.

"He'd call and we'd talk," Claire continued. "I knew his name was David, but he told me his last name was Kelley. Blond hair, blue-eyed Irish Catholic kid by all appearances. Why would I doubt it? The more we talked and hung out some, he opened up about his dad's death, and he told me he was actually a Kennedy and the Kelley's were family friends.

"David would pick me up from school sometimes in Nashville," Claire said. "I went to a girl's school and we wore little plaid skirts, white blouses and knee socks. Our skirts were actually quite short. He got a kick out of his 'little Catholic school girl."

Although his drug use was getting heavier, he was still able to relax and enjoy life. "He was a fun guy," Claire said. "We used to go hang out some at Percy Priest Lake. He loved being near the water. He was funny about it. He was so skinny that his ribs showed from his back. We got a little cat boat and went out on the water a few times. He liked to do that. David called it 'our good ole Catholic guilt'. He'd laugh and say, "at least we Catholics get together to sin so that the effect on the rest of the world is lessened."

David's closest friend in Nashville was Adell Crowe, a journalist with the Gannett News Service. She saw his vulnerability saying that "he was very aloof and kind of sad. This was right after the accident with the jeep, and I think he was working out a few things. But he was so fired up about the job. I'm surprised he didn't get into journalism more."

Despite his increasingly worrying use of narcotics, David still managed to graduate from Middlesex in the top third of his class. He started a Bachelor of Arts degree at Harvard in the autumn of 1974. Using history as his major, and with his Nashville experience under his belt, he hoped for a career in journalism.

"I met him at his home in VA the summer after he graduated high school," One friend stated. "He'd just returned from an internship at the Nashville Tennessean. He was really jazzed about journalism. We spent a lot of time together the following autumn, winter and spring in Cambridge...His pain over his father was still intense, and he wasn't close to his mom, which made losing his dad an even greater loss. He was using pretty heavily the entire time I knew him...David was smart, funny and almost hypersensitive. He was lost in the Kennedy mythos. He felt he didn't fit the image..."

"The first night David and I hung out," the friend recalled, "we were in a den type room at Hickory Hill, and there was this poster on the wall with a phrase that said something like the youth of our country is in the streets out of control. David said, "Guess who said that?" and I replied, "I don't know, your father? Your uncle?" Turned out it was a quote from Hitler. I was embarrassed beyond description, but David cracked up."

Journalist Tom Oliphant spent time with David during his Harvard years. They met during the summer of '74 when David had had worked as a journalist in DC. "He'd bring papers over to my apartment in Cambridge and we would generally talk about school and school subjects," Oliphant remembered. "Sometimes he'd come over and just sit. He was an excellent writer and he was doing work in school that was out-of-this-world good. He wasn't bookish, but he had an original and at times brilliant way of looking at things. But he was clearly in deep psychological trouble."

David had to contend with his siblings and cousins competing for academic excellence. "There was a lot of talent, drive and frustration under one tent," said a friend of RFK Sr. "That was certainly not the best thing for David."

"It was a classic case," said a family friend. "He hated almost everything connected with his family, but he wanted them to acknowledge his life."

He may have been shining academically, but his physical appearance wasn't winning him any awards. Beneath his unchanging attire of Levi jeans and un-ironed shirt, David was looking ill. "He was incredibly emaciated and white faced," one Harvard classmate remembered. "He was walking death."

Another, a woman who roomed above David at Winthrop House said that his routine, like his appearance, also varied very little day-to-day. "I never saw him without a Colt 45 Malt Liquor in one hand and a cigarette in the other, no matter what time of day it was," she said. "He looked fragile, kind of skeletal, with this terrible pallor. It was so at odds with that healthy Kennedy persona – touch football, sailing, beaches."

His drug use had steadily climbed since the jeep accident, and was particularly noticeable during his tenure at Harvard. "I saw him become a tortured version of himself," one former classmate remembered. "He was an extraordinarily bright, extraordinarily unhappy guy. There was a grouchiness and contentiousness that was tied to his intellectual strength. He would argue almost any point. It would drive you nuts."

"David may have been the most brilliant of all the Kennedy children," another Harvard acquaintance said. "It was a raw intelligence...frightening in some ways...You could talk to him about literature, politics, damned near anything. When he was on his mind was razor sharp. But the addiction destroyed everything, the good included."

"Oh, my David, my sweet little David," Noelle Bombardier recalls fondly when asked about the youthful David Kennedy. "He really liked me and I liked him so much," Noelle stated. "Though he was so charming, he often acted strangely. For instance, he would use the bathroom without closing the door and I would walk by and holler at him and say, 'David! Please' But nothing bothered him. Yet at the same time, everything bothered him. At first, I didn't know what was wrong with him. I thought well, maybe he's just depressed. But it all came out from Ethel one day."

Noelle was asked to pick something up for Ethel but she didn't her car with her, so it would have to wait.

"Oh, is something wrong with your car?" Ethel asked.

"Well, actually, I let David use it to run an errand."

"What!"

"Don't worry, Mrs. Kennedy, he told me he would be back within half an hour."

"You should never have done that!" Ethel exclaimed in an alarmed tone. "Don't you know that the boy is on drugs?"

Momentarily stunned, Noelle apologized for allowing David to borrow her car.

"Well, you didn't know. It's not like we tell everyone! But now that you know, never let him drive Noelle. You must promise me!"

Noelle promised.

Just then, they heard a car approaching that promptly slammed on the brakes. It was David. He quickly entered the house, breathless and sweating and breezed past the two women.

"David Kennedy!" Ethel said, leaping from her chair. "Don't you dare ever ask Noelle for the keys to her car again. She didn't know that I don't want you driving, but you know it and you took advantage of her!"

Seemingly unfazed, he said, 'Oh Okay, cool, Mom." Looking across at Noelle, he then said he was sorry and flashed the famous Kennedy grin and disappeared to his room upstairs.

"Oh my God," Ethel said reseating herself. "Well, at least he didn't hurt himself, or anyone else."

"...In David's case, there was nothing to connect to the life," the friend continued. "Even free of the drug influence, there was a deep, overpowering sense of nihilism in his personality. No person, no job, no hobby could give him something to plug into."

Lawford: "Sometime in the fall of 1974 the FBI got a tip from one of their informants, who happened to be a Hell's Angel that a particularly nasty chapter of the motorcycle gang was planning to kidnap a Kennedy. The informant didn't know which Kennedy, so on a crisp fall day in Boston, my cousins Joe, Bobby and David got their very own Secret Service details. What these motorcycle geniuses thought they were going to get by kidnapping one of my cousins I have no idea, but I knew that if they took Joe, Bobby or David they were going to get a handful......David offered to have 'one of my guys drop you off at school, if you want.'

'No thanks, man. I can drive myself.'

"Then, 'Hey man, it's too bad you didn't get a detail of your own. We could have a football game. Me and my guys against you and your guys.'

"David was a master of rubbing your nose in it. 'Yeah, man, too bad.'

"It turned out that the reason for my tardy detail was that the brain surgeon bikers who were going to kidnap a Kennedy thought that Ethel Kennedy was married to Peter Lawford.

"My cousins and I figured that if these Hell's Angel's idiots couldn't get who was married to whom right, we weren't in much danger. So we just enjoyed the extra bodies for touch football."

David's adolescence was coming to an end. His journalistic career had gotten off to a promising start and he was doing well at Harvard. Would it continue however, with the growing expectation and an even more escalating drug habit?

PART 3: WITH A ROLL OF THE DICE
1975 - 1979

10. NASHVILLE '75

As David left his teens and moved into his twenties, those closest to him had yet to reach the point of desperation over his drug use. However, concerns were growing. While they saw that he was excelling in his studies at Harvard and had started tentatively on his professional path, they also noticed his increasing use of narcotics. The later would come to be a dominant theme in the last half of the 70s – acquiring it, problems associated with abusing it and of course getting off it. The next period of his life was the most distressing and unsettling for David – his recklessness and risk taking appeared to be limitless. David would be faced with a hard question: Would he try and overcome his addiction and find his path or would he gamble with his life with increasingly bad odds? For the time being, he chose to continue to roll the dice.

The second half the 1970s opens with David looking to develop his journalistic skills. He had spent four months during the spring and early summer of '74 as an intern for the newspaper. The then editor, John Seigenthaler had been close friends with RFK. As David impressed staff during his first tenure, he was welcomed back when he expressed an interest in returning. A Newsweek article published shortly after his death captured his life that summer of '75 quite well:

"I temporary: that was David, careering between summer jobs and aborted semesters, briefly loved women and halt-formed dreams. One foray took him to Fort Lauderdale, to work for family friend and flamboyant businessman John Jay Hooker, whom he knew from Nashville. But David never did work on that aimless journey. He slept until the early afternoons, whiled away the days around Hooker's pool and marshaled his energy only to organize a junket to a Rolling Stones concert in Memphis that summer. He was 20 then, but he daydreamed liked a small boy, repeatedly telling the story of how his father had once rescued him from a treacherous undertow in the Malibu surf. And how, late that very night, he had watched his father die."

Behind Blue Eyes

His rather contented summer was interrupted when he unwittingly found himself part of the headlines. On July 13th, 1975, David decided to have a quick trip back to Hickory Hill. He bought a second hand 1974 Toyota sports car and started out on his journey heading in the north-easterly direction that would take him to McLean, VA.

He got as far as Woodstock, VA before being pulled over for doing 92 mph (148 km/hr) along interstate 81. He was charged with reckless driving and for failing to have a driver's license or registration.

The new wave of publicity came at a bad time for the Kennedy family, who were trying to lie low with the 7th anniversary of the Chappaquiddick tragedy fresh in people minds. The matter came before the court on the very day of the anniversary.

Magistrate David Cook, a 31 year-old Vietnam veteran and Kennedy admirer, said that he went to considerable trouble for David. Rather than issue a jail warrant, Cook released David on his own recognizance after just over an hour. The Virginia police accommodated David's request for no media intrusion, through a series of near elaborate decoys. 26 year-old Russell McGuire, A local photographer with the Woodstock North Virginian Daily, complained at the preferential treatment David appeared to receive, sparking comparisons to Ted post Chappaquiddick.

"When the Virginia trooper called him Mr. Kennedy and complies with his wishes to obfuscate the press," McGuire said, "Then I am amazed. Because anybody else, 20 years old and looking like that would have been called a wild-eyed hippie."

However, David was said to be calm and well behaved and happily complied with the requests of the police. He seemed unperturbed by his plight.

McGuire, who was at the police station when David was brought in, saw the young man "sitting on a chair cross-legged, serenely reading his People magazine…with the long hair and tennis shoes, sparkling white. He wore blue denim jeans, I think, and a sports shirt. He looked like a class-A hippie, alright."

Not having any ID on him, David used the People magazine article, which featured a picture of him with his brother Joe and Mohammed Ali to prove his identity. David unknowingly was creating something of a stir in the county police station.

"The Kennedy magic was in the air," McGuire said. "People were whispering and giggling and fussing over the whole the whole thing. He was absolutely bemused or completely indifferent to what was going on."

The photo of him with Mohammed Ali (which seems to have been lost to history) triggered a comment from David that Ali was the "world's greatest boxer" and would win his rematch with George Foreman and his rationale for thinking so. His words were said to have carried a fair weight to them.

After a few telephone calls that proved the veracity of his identity and that he was licensed and insured, he was free to go. Maguire positioned himself out the front of the jail, expecting a scoop of a lifetime. He had the shot already to go – the antique sign "Shenandoah County Jail" at the top of the frame and presumably the disgraced David below it. As a bevy of Woodstock's finest emerged from the front door, McGuire waited for his subject. But the police were decoys – the newsmaker had slipped out the back and into the night.

He was fined $50 plus court costs on Friday, September 26. He did not have to make an appearance. It would be a pattern that was to be repeated several times over the next few years.

David arrived back in Nashville with the question of what to do about the incident. David called Seigenthaler to discuss the situation. The editor said David was adamant – the story must be told.

"He told me that he expected me to live by my 'no special favors order and to run the story," Seigenthaler recalled. "I did. That tells you something about David's character."

Wayne Whitt said he was surprised that David didn't return to Nashville after '75, considering his obvious journalistic skills. "He was very interested in journalism," Whitt said. "But he never came back us. I believe his problems started after he left here..."

When he wasn't busy creating the bylines – in one way or another – he would delve into another passion: American history. He was particularly fascinated with his dad's life and would enjoy researching and uncovering both his written and oral work. "He was big on knowing his dad's speeches and some of the lesser publicized works he gave," Claire revealed.

"His taste in literature ran to biographies. "He seemed to be drawn towards Gonzo style writings," Claire thought. "He had read Salinger, Hunter Thompson (a family friend) and Hemingway. He liked the 'screw the world' lifestyles they seem to have. I always wondered if he was trying to emulate them at times. Almost like, 'if I can be like Daddy then I'll be the opposite', but it hurt like hell for letting him down. We had a love of history in common, and he was fairly well read for a teenager in those days."

Characterized since birth as the runt of the litter, and though it occurred relatively late, David began to have a major growth spurt between his 19th and 21st birthdays. He arrived in Nashville a modest 5'9" (identical to his father) with few expecting any more height to come his way. Two years later, however, he had grown no less than five inches to a gangly 6'2." He would now be eye-level with the tallest of the RFK offspring.

"He had really grown," Claire confirmed. "But thin as always." She thought David's slimness further accentuated his height. A somewhat stooped appearance when depressed gave him the look of someone carrying the weight of the world on his shoulders.

11. The Pull of the Undertow

David had barely gotten back to Hickory Hill from Nashville, when he was off again. A party of seven, very much led by Bobby jr, ventured to Rio Apurimac in Peru for three weeks during August '75. Bobby had hoped to recapture the Kennedy mystique by venturing into 300 miles (480 km) of unexplored river. He would be the focal point as his father had been on earlier, happy rafting adventures. The trip Bobby envisaged was no picnic as it had been in the 60s. Bobby wanted to make a grand statement that he had arrived as Kennedy and was ready for the challenges destiny had in store for him.

For his part, David saw the trip as his "big brother's own personal heart of darkness." He watched from the sidelines, refusing to work or show an interest in the adventure. He came well stocked with books and cigarettes, the latter of which he rationed out to the others in place of his responsibilities.

They arrived back in time for the annual RFK Pro-Celebrity Tennis Tournament, where anxious family members all gathered. "Nobody in the family had heard from us for close to three weeks," Chris Lawford stated, "and there was great concern as to whether we were still alive...Bobby, David, Lem and I made our entrance into (the Plaza Hotel in New York) like the conquering heroes we felt we were. It was quite dramatic, and for the moment we were adored. But only for a moment..."

Whatever good will and relief there was on David's safe return from the wilds of South America soon vanished. The relationship with his mother and his other family members went back to being strained. At Aspen for Christmas, while the others engaged in the winter activities, David appeared disorientated and disinterested.

Ethel "just tore into David sometimes," a family friend said. "I remember once she misplaced two hundred dollars. She came in and immediately began accusing David. He told her it was ridiculous – he had money, what did he need two hundred dollars for? She just kept it up, absolutely vicious, wouldn't let him go."

Filmmaker Bob Rafelson saw David looking rather downcast as he hung out with Hunter Thompson. He didn't see the family support that insiders say was present. He recalls telling Bobby Jr of his concerns for his brother.
"He was at the top of his game," Rafelson said of RFK jr. "writing a book about some Alabama judge, and doing these little macho tricks, doped up and talking about falconing and politics. I steered the conversation around to his brother David and said I thought he was awfully sickly looking, on the verge of

really going under. Bobby thought about it for a minute and said 'yes, somebody ought to wean David away from Hunter' who he said was a bad influence. But then he was off again, talking about something else. David didn't seem to be a high priority for him or anybody else."

"To be so alone, to be so bereft of anything that's going to help you in life...it's more than many of us can overcome," a friend concluded. "...There always was that look in his eyes of someone who is mortally wounded."

"He was intentionally slovenly, especially when he had to be presentable," Author Harrison Rainie observed. "He used his sardonic humor as a cutting weapon – except that he'd often get cut up in the fights it provoked."

To some friends, David appeared withdrawn and temperamental. They were never quite sure what side of David they would encounter.

"He was extremely moody," a Washington acquaintance said. "You never knew what to expect. Yes there was a demon in him. And try as he might, he couldn't get rid of it. He wanted to so badly. I thought that was obvious."

"He was highly competitive and could have a mean streak," Claire says of another of David's less desirable traits. "He played me in Tennis at the club one day. The first two sets he was obviously my boyfriend. We went to have a coke and some guy made a snide comment to him about playing like a pussy. When we went back on the court, he absolutely annihilated me. He was so competitive and so into the macho thing at that point that me crying and being really upset because he was slamming that ball at me had no effect on him. He told me to suck it up and stop being a baby. Another 'fun' thing about him."

While regarded as a superb natural athlete, arguably the best in the family, he didn't always play by the rules.

"David was certainly not a good sport at any point," one friend remembered. "When he was losing at football, he would deliberately kick or punch someone to make them give up the ball."

Top: David as the new addition to the RFK family, 1955 © Jacques Lowe/JFK Library
Bottom: RFK family at Hickory Hill, 1957 © LIFE

Behind Blue Eyes

Top: 2-year-old David with "Meegan" 6/27/57 © Bettman / Corbis
Bottom: RFK kids on the CBS TV show "Person to Person" 9/13/57 (c) CBS Photo Archive / Hulton Archive

Top: David and his dad at Hickory Hill, 1957. © LIFE
Bottom: David with his parents and older sister Kathleen, 1957 © LIFE

Behind Blue Eyes

Top: Bedtime prayers at Hickory Hill, 1957 (c) Jacques Lowe / JFK LIbrary
Bottom: Joseph and Rose Kennedy with some their grandchildren, 1957 (David sitting on his grandmother's lap.)

A special bond: Bobby and David, 1958, © Jacques Lowe / JFK LIbrary

Behind Blue Eyes

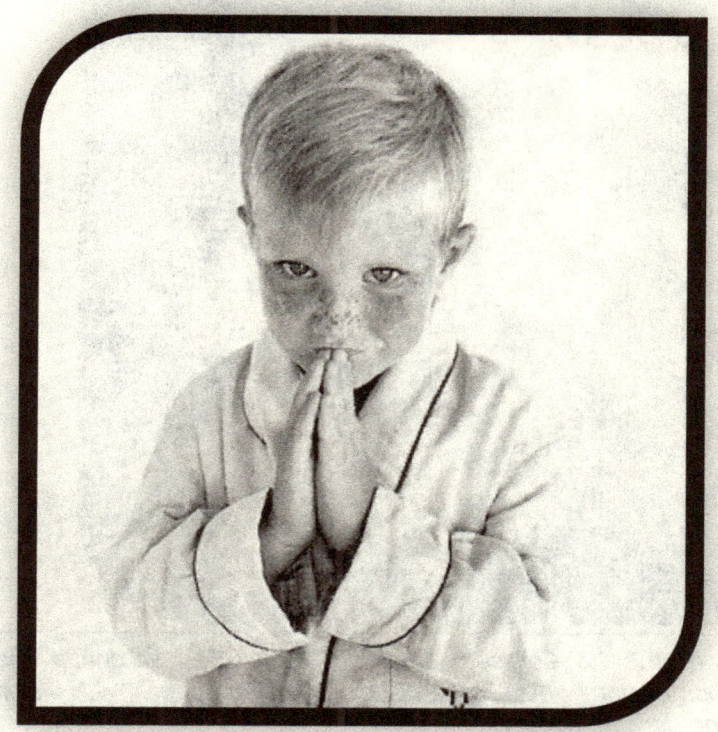

4 year old David © Jacques Lowe / JFK Library

Top: David at the LA Coliseum July 15, 1960. JFK, accepting the democratic nomination, would make his New Frontier speech - his vision for the coming decade. © LIFE
Bottom: President-elect JFK with his Vice-President LBJ outside JFK's house in Georgetown with RFK jr and David – November 27, 1960 © AP

Behind Blue Eyes

David in the spring of 1961 in a photo taken by his Aunt Jackie. JFK had inscribed the photo with "A future President inspects his property."
In 1984, shortly before his death, Paula Scully unearthed the photo and said that it "put a big smile" on David's face.
© LIFE

Eight-year-old David at play at Hyannis Port – August 29, 1963.

Next page:
Top left: Christmas 1963. © Jacques Lowe / JFK Library
Top right: Hickory Hill, June 1964 © LIFE
Bottom: During RFK's successful senatorial campaign, autumn 1964. (TV still)

Behind Blue Eyes

When RFK ran for the presidency, 12-year-old David was the only offspring to remain unenthusiastic. "He should have known he was going to be shot," he angrily said later. "And he should have cared about what that was going to do to us."

Top: David and younger brother Michael, 10, at Vanderbilt University listening to their father, RFK, during a campaign speech, March 21, 1968. © Jimmy Ellis / Nashville Tennessean.

Bottom: Easter 1968. It was this photo that was splashed across the newspapers after his first brush with the law the same year. © AP

However it may have looked to outsiders, people who know the family has said they always hung in there. They never gave up on David, however problematic the relationship with him may be.

"It's important they know should they get into trouble," Ethel said of her children in 1981, "they've got an anchor back home that's never going to move no matter what happens and that they'll always have that."

In addition to annual summer trips, she would even drag him to tennis courts in order to get him involved in activities. "She was always trying to draw him out," one Washington insider stated. "She never gave up on the kid, but there were times of despair. He would go back to the habit, and she would throw up her hands and ask, "What can we do about David?"

A friend of Ted Kennedy's said that the Senator also tried to help David as his drug abuse became more serious. "People reached out to him for the rest of his life," the friend said. "Ted Kennedy was there a lot. His brothers and sisters and cousins all tried. But they could never really reach him. Something had clicked."

One such way his Uncle Ted tried to help, was by employing him as an intern in his senatorial office in Boston after David took a semester off in 1975. His job included filing and doing case work. He would do the rounds with Teddy as he attended lunches and receptions. He even sat in on meetings. The Senator had hoped it would spark an enthusiasm for public service by learning the ropes the way David's father and Uncle Jack had done. A Ted Kennedy staffer remembered the time fondly. "David was an able and exceptionally kind and compassionate young man."

His eldest brother Joe, though less than 3 years his senior, would periodically take it upon himself to be something of David's protector. "Look at him," he said to a friend as David lay in a stupor one day. "He was a varsity halfback as a sophomore (in high school) – something none of the rest of us could do. He was terrific. And now he can barely put one leg in front of the other."

A friend said that Bobby Jr would help David in other ways. "Bobby would shoot up David," he said. "His hand was too shaky to do it himself, so his brother would do it for him. Of course, he introduced David to it. He was the leader of the pack. David was emulating him."

"He seemed very disorientated at times," Claire told this author, "but as a whole, he was his usual cuttingly witty self...He was an extremely smart guy. He wasn't as together as he could have been, but who can blame him? He was very self-deprecating."

Though still only twenty years old at the beginning of 1976, David's drug use was starting to cause his health to suffer. His Uncle Sargent Shriver, married to Eunice, had announced his candidacy for the presidency and it typically became a whole family enterprise - minus one member. Though the bid was ultimately brief and unsuccessful, David chose to spend that time shooting heroin, with only a near fatal infection halting the relentless pursuit of oblivion. He was stoned every day for six full weeks until early March. One day Bobby's friends Eric Breindel and Peter Kaplan discovered David passed out in his room at Winthrop House at Harvard. They rushed him to Massachusetts General Hospital with a raging fever on March 4. Doctors immediately diagnosed bacterial endocarditis, an infection of the inner lining of the heart and its valves. David contracted it through using dirty needles. There were other complications.

Twenty days after admission, the media announced that David was being treated for Pneumonia in his upper lungs and would require a lengthy stay in the hospital. The condition improved with antibiotics but he started complaining of stomach pains. Doctors originally thought he had a case of appendicitis but weren't certain. So on April 16, more than 6 weeks after first being admitted doctors performed exploratory surgery on David.

"It was safer to perform exploratory surgery," said hospital spokesman Martin Bander at the time, "than to risk the very serious complications of appendicitis." Doctors realized that an inflamed lymph gland had resulted from the antibiotics.

He had a private room in Phillips House at Mass. Gen. For his extended stay. The family rallied. "At first there was the usual outpouring of concern," David remembered. "We Kennedys aren't much for the day-in, day-out thing, but we sure put out in a crisis. My mother was there, Teddy, Joe, somebody pretty much around the clock."

"She's a very complicated, intense person," said one friend on Ethel. "When her kids fall down, she's there. She's an angel of mercy. But nobody can sustain an angel posture for very long. When David was hospitalized...you've never seen a hospital room filled with more sunshine, with more guests, with more steaks brought in, more round-the-clock visits by any mother, more laughs, more videocassettes, more anything. There was this great bulk of kindness, and then she would depart and be gone."

"Ethel is 100 percent for her children in some areas," said a friend of David, "but she doesn't understand them always, and what she doesn't understand, she doesn't want to hear about."

Ethel employed her usual strategy when she was concerned about David – she planned another trip for him. Given the gravity of the situation, an adventure to the lettuce fields of California would clearly not suffice. A far flung destination seemed more appropriate.

"They said I needed activity to keep my mind off things," David said of his foray to Pakistan. "Actually, they needed me gone so I wouldn't annoy them."

David was accompanied by Doug Spooner, who remembered wild boar shooting with General Zia shortly after touching down in Pakistan.

"We were in helicopters with M16s, honorary members of the Pakistani Rangers," Spooner recalled. "It took us all day and half the night to get a boar but finally we did. While we were up in Peshawar looking at the Kyber Pass, Gaddafi arrived in Pakistan. Bhutto got the idea that it would be good for a Gaddafi and a Kennedy to meet. So he had Gaddafi fly up and we met him and had this brief conversation. Gaddafi's entourage was extremely nervous, jumping to anticipate his every need. Afterward we flew out of Peshawar in a staff plane behind Gaddafi. A lot of his people were on the plane with us. One of them came up and asked David what he thought of their leader. David gave them his drug grin and said, 'Well, I think the guy's a little unpredictable.' Every Libyan in the plane began to laugh hysterically."

David was back briefly to start the fall semester at Harvard but dropped out. He would spend most of his time at Hickory Hill, but would regularly spend a couple of days in New York with friends.

"David was Mrs. Kennedy least favorite," recalled Noelle Bombardier. "He was an embarrassment to her. He kept his room in the house, but she couldn't have cared less whether she talked to him or not, whether he ate dinner with her or not. At dinnertime she'd say to the children, 'ok it's ready,' and she'd make certain everyone was at the table with her. But she didn't do that with David. If there was any company, she'd tell David to go upstairs, like a child."

"Of course, Mrs. Kennedy was very, very worried about him," Noelle stated. "But she was also embarrassed. I recall one afternoon when Princess Grace Kelly was coming to visit Hickory Hill...Mrs. Kennedy had planned a wonderful luncheon. Meanwhile, David was walking around high or drunk, or...really, I didn't know what was going on with him, but he definitely wasn't right, stumbling and bumping into the furniture. Mrs. Kennedy was frantic about it and finally said, 'Okay, look, Noelle, first things first. We have to get him out of here. We don't have time to do anything else!' I called the senator and he said, 'Okay, bring him over here to my house.' He lived just down the street on Cambridge Road. So I got David into the car, drove over there, and dropped him off. 'Tell Ethie I'll take it from here,' the senator told me as he took David. Then I raced back to Hickory Hill just as Princess Grace and her siblings were arriving. We had our lovely afternoon though it was quite disconcerting knowing what was secretly going on behind the scenes. Mrs. Kennedy was practically jumping out of her skin the entire time. Finally, Princess Grace and her family members left. Within seconds of their walking out the door, Mrs. Kennedy said, 'Okay, go get David and bring him back.' So I raced back to the senator's house, he handed David back to me, and I brought him home."

"Because Ethel refused to allow David to use any of the family cars, or to give him pocket money," Jerry Oppenheimer writes, "he'd beg the help for both, then drive across the Potomac in a borrowed car to score heroin with borrowed money. Other times he'd leave for a day or two to buy drugs in New York. Most, if not all, of the staff at Hickory Hill, having had no experience with drug addiction, thought that David was an alcoholic."

The beginning of the New Year 1977, started inauspiciously. He once again made the news for a traffic violation. On Tuesday, January 25th, at about 1 a.m., David was driving through Arlington, MA, when he was charged with a number of infringements: running through a stop sign, driving without a license in an unregistered, uninsured car. He appeared at Cambridge District Court on February 17 to answer the charges. He was found guilty on two of the four, running the stop sign and not having a license and after pleading guilty, was fined $20.

Three months later David again made the headlines. This time however it was positive news. On May 29th, his Uncle Jack would have celebrated his sixtieth birthday. The family sent him to JFK's birth house in Beals Street, Brookline as the Kennedy representative for the celebrations. Both he and family friend Dave Powers spoke to the gathering, numbering more than 100 people. Although nervous about his public speaking abilities, he greatly impressed his audience with his warmth and grace, however overawed by the spotlight he appeared.

"He was overwhelmed by the family's fame," former girlfriend thought, "but if he wanted something sometimes he'd use the Kennedy card. Usually he'd just want to be himself and deal with his own crap."

One day in Boston David found more serious trouble, though out of the public eye on this occasion. He would frequent the seedy Roxbury area in his quest to cross darker boundaries.

"My father was concerned about blacks in one way," David commented, "and I was concerned about them in another – as people from whom I could get drugs."

He was told by a dealer that a drugs transaction would take place in a public toilet. When David arrived, the dealer tied him up and produced a knife which he used to cut David along his abdomen. The wound was only superficial, which disappointed him.

"I was modeling myself on the James Caan character in The Gambler," David said. "I saw that movie over and over. I loved the last scene, where Caan had finally pushed things so far that the black guy cut his face, and then he goes to the mirror and sees the wound and smiles. I could relate to that."

"His father's death scarred him," Said a woman friend of David's. "And he seemed attracted to the pain the felt." It was his one constant in his ever changing world of variables. "When you lose so many people that you love, what kind of message does that deliver?" a friend asked. "He couldn't count on anything, and he was afraid to love. But when he shot that heroin into his veins, he felt, 'I know what this is doing to me.' It was a guarantee…"

At the behest of his family, David began seeing a psychiatrist. Lee B. Macht (1937-1981) was mainly known for his role as chief of psychiatry at Cambridge City Hospital. He was also a lecturer in psychiatry at the Harvard Medical School. In 1975 Macht he was appointed Commissioner of Mental Health for Massachusetts. In 1978, President Jimmy Carter appointed him to the President's Commission on Mental Health. He would treat David until September 1979 and himself die prematurely in April 1981 at the age of 43.

It was evident David needed far more urgent attention, but the family appeared at a loss as to how to help or what form that help should take.

Ted and Ethel sat down with him hoping to find the key to unlock him from his struggles. "What do we have to do, David?" Ted asked him in an almost pleading tone. "What is that you need from us? Because we don't know what to do. You tell me and I'll do it, David. Just tell me."

"I want you to bring back my dad, how about that?" David said angrily. "How about *that*, Uncle Teddy. Can you do *that?*"

His mother and uncle just looked at each sadly and as Ted shook his head, David stood up, "I didn't think so," and left the room.

Instead of traveling to rehab, he traveled to Europe during the summer. He soon returned (and to old ways). Things were reaching crisis point, and while the alarm bells seemed to be finally ringing for his family, no one knew how to stop them.

One reason for the Kennedys' collective tentativeness was to do with his sometimes violent and often unpredictable behavior when drunk or high, one friend suggested.

"His cries for help were largely ignored because he would lash out at anyone who would come near and tried to help him," the friend said.

"It was as though he didn't want to be helped," the friend thought. "He wanted to destroy himself as quickly as possible. He was prone to violent, unprovoked attacks on his brothers and sisters or anybody else who got in his way.

"He would react very violently to frustration," the friend furthered. "Once at Hickory Hill, his younger brother Michael took the last beer out of the fridge. David went berserk and slugged him.

"The one time he would really shine would be when he recited his father's poems, but he would quickly turn bitter and morose," the friend concluded.

A man claiming to be David's drug dealer came forward and shed light on David's life at this difficult juncture.

"I was David Kennedy's heroin connection in Harlem," the man claimed. "I made several hundred purchases of heroin and sometimes cocaine for David."

The dealer says he was working as a security guard (when not pushing drugs) at a private methadone clinic in New York when he met David.

"He was using an alias – Stephen Fasandola – but I recognized him straight away from his pictures in the newspaper. He'd come in every few days for his methadone supply," the dealer recalled. "He was taking methadone the way most junkies do: as a heroin supplement. He was still using heroin."

One day David gave the dealer a ride in his car and asked him to buy heroin and cocaine for him.

"Basically I was Kennedy's middleman," the dealer stated. "Because of the knifing in Roxbury, he was afraid to make buys of junk himself...But he never shot up in front of me," the man added.

His drug addiction brought him perilously close to death at this time. On April 27th, 1978, he bought an ounce (28 grams) of cocaine, with the intention of selling it. He decided to use some of it himself, and shot it with Dilaudid, a morphine derivative. His girlfriend at the time came home and saw David unconscious and called Doug Spooner who immediately rushed him to Massachusetts General. The newspapers again noted David's admission for "pneumonia."

He slowly rallied – again. But things almost immediately went back to being chaotic. He didn't have to venture into the bowels of the "hood" to find high drama. It seemed to shadow him – cloak his life wherever he went.

"Oh my God, something terrible has happened," Gertrude Ball told the Hickory Hill Day staff one day during the summer of '78. "We have to call the police." Gertrude Ball worked at the Kennedy owned Park Agency in New York. She was with Supreme Court Justice, William O. Douglas. They both rushed over to Hickory Hill upon hearing of a break-in.

David told them that a man had broken in through the third-floor window where David was sleeping. After an apparent bloody struggle, the intruder fled.

Noelle Bombardier went upstairs to check David's story – she was suspicious. "The window was broken, the room had been turned upside down and there was blood on the floor," she said later. "There also were needles and vials on the floor. It was now ten o'clock in the morning and David was in his bed sleeping with a girl and I couldn't wake up either one of them. I went downstairs and said to Gertrude Ball and Justice Douglas, 'Please don't call the police. This was not the work of a burglar. This was David's doing. This was drugs.'"

Bombardier said she contacted Ethel at Hyannis Port. "I told her what had happened. I told her that it was really David, not a burglar; that David must have been looking for drugs or shooting drugs and that he'd probably freaked out. She didn't say a word. Then I asked what she wanted us to do. She said, 'Go tell David to clean the room.' I said, 'I beg your pardon?' I told her that David was asleep with a girl next to him. She said, 'Well, you go and tell David to clean his room.' I thought to myself, 'What the hell good is that going to do? This poor kid is sick.' So I told her it might be better for me to have David call her after he got up, but that I wasn't about to tell him to clean the room like he was a five-year-old. Besides, if I tried he'd probably punch me in the face. I told her Gertrude Ball and Justice Douglas were there and wanted to call the police. That really upset her. She said, 'No, no, no, no, no. Don't call the police whatever you do! I just want to make sure that David goes and cleans up his own mess.' Mrs. Kennedy then asked to talk to Gertrude Ball and told her the same thing, have David clean the room, don't call the police."

After quickly ushering the Supreme Court Justice out of the house, Noelle called Ted Kennedy, to inform him of the latest David-related drama.

"Holy Christ!" he responded. "I told Ethie he needs to be in a hospital. There's nothing else I can do," Ted sadly lamented.

He was ordered to stay at his uncle's house. "I promise to be a good boy," David told Ted. "I promise I won't get into any trouble." He was only at Ted's, a few miles away, for two days.

"My Uncle's as bad as I am," David said. "He needs a babysitter more than I do! He can't do anything for me..." He was back at Hickory Hill only one day when he took one of Ethel's credit cards and left for New York.

"You know I tried to get him to stay..." Ted told Noelle Bombardier. "But he wouldn't do it. What should we do now?"

It appeared no one had the answers.

Ethel blew up when Noelle informed her of David's departure. "Mrs. Kennedy had called me at Hickory Hill and demanded to know where David was," Noelle recalled. "She said, 'I told you to watch him.' I told Mrs. Kennedy that there was only so much I could do. I told her quite bluntly that if she couldn't control her son, how was I supposed to do it? She said, 'How could you let him use my credit card? Where did he get the money to go to New York? Did you loan him money?' She was so pissed off at me that she wanted to come home and blow my brains out."

Ted appeared shortly afterwards, looking noticeably concerned. "If and when you hear from David," Ted said to Noelle, "makes sure he calls us."

David returned to Hickory Hill after three days in New York, but refused to stay at Ted's house. In Noelle Bombardier's presence, the Senator telephoned Ethel at the compound. "There's nothing I can do," he repeated an earlier comment. "You'll have to put him in a hospital."

David was now referring to his family as the Committee to Keep David Out of the Picture." They persuaded him to let his sister Kathleen become his guardian. He was sent to McLeans, a psychiatric hospital in Belmont, a suburb of Boston at the beginning of October.

"It looked like the Ritz on the outside and the Snake pit on the inside," David remembered. "The first thing I saw when I went in there was a guy on all fours barking like a dog, literally. That's when I knew I was in trouble."

Kathleen saw the conditions her little brother endured and promised to have him out that day. She returned three days later with bad news – he'd be going nowhere. "The others say not to trust you," she told David. "That you'll say anything to get out. It turned out to be a longer stay. The family had not been idle for those three weeks of David's incarceration however. A radical step was proposed.

12. The Lost Son Finds England

Lord Harlech (1918-1985) had been a close personal friend of the Kennedys and Scottish surgeon, Dr. Margaret (Meg) Patterson (1922-2002) had successfully treated his drug addicted daughter. While locked up in McLeans, the Kennedy family approached him to try and get Dr. Patterson to help

David, who to say the least, was unimpressed with the latest strategy – despite their obvious good intentions. He thought it just a way for the family to get rid of him.

Margaret Ingram was the youngest of five children born in Aberdeen, Scotland to a comfortably off railway official. Brought up in a strict Christian household, the academically brilliant Patterson graduated from her private school Dux of the Year at just 16, and studied medicine at Aberdeen University, graduating as a doctor at twenty-one, having being awarded first prize in surgery, one of the youngest women to achieve that feat.

Her first job, the backdrop to which was the Second World War, was as a house surgeon at the Royal Hospital for Sick Children in home city. During her 12 months there, her interest in pain-relief to suffering children sparked a life-long interest in addiction studies. By twenty-five she added the highly prestigious degree Fellowship of the Royal College of Surgeons in Edinburgh University (FRCS) to her increasingly impressive resume, the only woman in the 100 person course.

Following twenty-five years in various places in the Far East, and a marriage to fellow Scot George Patterson (known as Patla) in 1953, the now Dr. Patterson returned to London in the early 1970s with knowledge in Chinese elctro-acupuncture which she was keen to further develop in the treatment for addiction. She became known for treating several high profile rock stars and other celebrities including Keith Richards from the Rolling Stones and Pete Townsend from the Who. The later became a strong advocate for her treatment. She would later be awarded an MBE.

"I was asked by Lord Harlech if I could possibly treat the drug-addicted son of the late Robert Kennedy...as a matter of critical urgency...The Kennedy family had tried everything and everybody, and they knew from Lord Harlech (of my previous successes) and they pleaded with him to use his influence with me to treat (David).

"But the problem was further complicated by the fact not only was the family internationally known, but there were political and financial implications which the media would love to exploit. They had put (David) into a mental institution for the time being because he was threatening to cause them political embarrassment in his demands for access to his inherited money, but this was a crisis measure and very secret.

"I told Lord Harlech...the fact that, even if were agreed to have David as a house guest by the strict Christian family with whom were living temporarily, they would have to know the identity of the patient." The lack of firm discipline, Dr. Meg believed in the house, and the views of the Pentecostal –type Christians would be seen as "Martian-like" to David.

"According to Lord Harlech, David's increasing drug addiction had so worried the Kennedy family...that they contrived with psychiatrists to have him admitted to a mental institution to keep him away from the media – and away from his grandfather, Joseph Kennedy's multi-million dollar inheritance. The problem with this act of incarceration was that it was both medically and legally questionable. So, the Kennedys wanted him out of the mental institution and out of the country and away from the media under strict supervision as soon as possible...In addition, they would send him to England accompanied by the Kennedy bodyguard to make sure that he got there and stayed there!"

David touched down in the UK in late October 1978. Upon arrival at his accommodation – 10 miles (16 km) south of Haywards Heath in Sussex, he made it clear that he had no intention of staying and that he was only there as his alternative was the mental institution. He told his hosts that he intended to sue his family as soon as he could call a lawyer.

He made quite a first impression – unfortunately a poor one. Things were off to a rocky start. "He was suffering from withdrawals," Dr Meg stated. "He smoked one cigarette after another, he swore profanely in almost every sentence, and was unbelievably rude. He was unmanageable."

Basing her treatment on her unique experiences in India and China, Dr. Meg formulated what she called NeuroElectric Therapy. It required the addicted person to wear an IPod like device as it transmitted signals to the brain. It was hoped that by doing so it would restore metabolic balance.

Dr. Patterson told David he would stay only on her terms and that he should give her his passport. The bodyguard was told to head back to the United States – he would not be needed.

"David went ballistic," Dr Patterson recalled, "refusing these terms with the foulest language imaginable. There was no way his conduct could be tolerated in any circumstances. And Patla in his inimitable manner finally spelled that out in words and phrases that rendered David speechless. Patla was a disciplinarian and a journalist, and had trawled the gutters of Asia for many years; there was nothing an immature twenty-three-year old junkie could do to stem him in full flow."

Before leaving to head home, the bodyguard told David to shape up; otherwise it was straight back to McLeans. It was a turning point in David's attitude.

"David sullenly accepted the inevitable, and submitted himself to the NET treatment with the minimal possible co-operation," Dr. Patterson stated. "He refused to be normally pleasant at the dining table, boorishly smoked without asking permission, recklessly talked about his famous family's indiscretions before the horrified Christian hosts, and openly mocked their religious practices."

David threatened to make telephone calls and expose Lord Harlech and the Patterson's as cranks, as well as revealing his family secrets to the media. However, his isolation coupled with the fact the husband worked from home made getting access to the phone difficult – but David tried.

"In his daily counseling sessions he poured out his grievances against the Kennedy family," Dr. Meg remembered. "All the inner–family secrets of their activities and aspirations; who among his siblings and relatives were taking the same and more drugs as he was without rebuke or retribution. He said because he was an adult 23 years of age, and spoke out against some of the activities and all of the hypocrisies that affected him, as a family they had connived at putting him away in a mental institution illegally rather than let him spend his grandfather's legacy to him by going to hell in a hand-basket if he so chose."

At the end of the first week, with David still refusing help and to co-operate, Patla made David a deal. If David did not contact the media and started to comply more willingly, he would be allowed a day in the coastal town of Brighton, 20 miles (32km) away, unsupervised. The Patterson's would also return to the United States and face the family with him, and if need be go to court to declare his mental competency.

When Ethel Kennedy phoned asking for her son and was told he was away from their supervision, the explosion was immediate. "...She burned up the telephone line," Dr. Patterson recalled. "She wanted to know what kind of irresponsible doctor I was, were we crazy, did we not realize what he was likely to do, and the damage he would cause if got to a telephone?

"...Eventually, Patla saw from my responses that I was being bombarded, and he took over," Dr. Meg furthered. "Pacing the floor, he informed her...that her twenty-three-year-old son was in danger of bringing death to himself and disgrace to the family because neither his father nor his mother had bothered to take the time to bring him up with a proper set of values. Did they only want us to keep him out of the way of the media to save their own embarrassment?" Patla, according to his wife's account, very firmly stood his ground and defended his wife's medical credentials and gave to straight back to David's mother.

Temper rising, Patla, told Ethel in effect to shut her mouth about things she had no knowledge. He said coldly that according to David she, "had not been able to control her own family in over twenty years, and we would return her son clean, cured and in his right mind in six weeks..."

That night the phone rang again with a Kennedy on the other end of the receiver. The Patterson's, who were asleep, looked at the clock – it was 1:30 a.m. David was calling from Brighton. It wasn't long either, before his temper began to match his mother's.

"Hello, is that you George?" David asked brightly.

"Yes," Patla said neutrally.

"George, you're not going to believe this," David continued.

"Try me," Patla said dryly.

"Well, I came down to Brighton to buy some music tapes, had a few beers and a meal, went to see a film and what do you know, I missed the last train.

"I can believe that," Patla said reasonably.

"Yeah, well, can you pick me up?" David asked, with assume casualness.

"No," said Patla.

"No?" David's voice rose incredulously. "What do you mean no?

"I mean no, I won't pick you up," Patla replied patiently.

"Then how do I get back?" David demanded.

"The same way as you got there," Patla replied.

"There are no more trains or buses running." David protested.

"You should have thought about that earlier," Patla said. "Before you left Haywards Heath Station, or at Brighton Station, in the several hours you had to make the decision. That's what sensible people do.

"It's too late for all that shit now!" David shouted angrily. Don't fuck me around man!"

"Take a taxi," Patla suggested reasonably.

"I've no money left," David said less confidently.

"Then hitch-hike," Patla answered. "It's only twenty miles."

"It's raining," David said sullenly.

"That's England," Patla said understandingly. "It was in the weather forecast if you listened."

"Come on man," David urged, sensing a softening. "You can be here in thirty minutes."

"No way," Patla said firmly. "You chose not to discuss your plans with me or Meg, so now you take responsibility for your decisions. You spent your money in the way you wanted, you spent the time in the way you wanted, which is fine by me. All normal people do that. Just take the consequences, like we all do. And while you wait for the hitch-hike, or walking back, think over whether it was worth it. That's what all non-junkies do all the time. Here endeth the first lesson. See you sometime."

""You..."

Patla hung up the phone and went back to sleep.

David made it back after four hours and three hitches. He was allowed to sleep in, and surfaced at noon to announce he was leaving immediately. He ordered the Patterson's to phone his family to have them meet him. He was done with his treatment, he said.

"Sit down shithead," Patla told David matter-of-factly that afternoon. "You're not going anywhere, or doing anything. You have no money and we're not giving you any. When you leave here, you will either be cured, or you will be escorted to the mental institution with your bodyguard. If you chose to walk away now and take the consequences, that's fine with us. We just telephone your decision to your family. We took you in to do one thing: to cure you of your addiction. You stay on that machine until Meg declares you detoxified, and you stay close to me until I say that you are fit to live with. Your problem, like all your kind, is not drugs; it's monomania. You are a foul-mouthed, rude, spoiled, ill-mannered, dirty, selfish, and despicable lout! Millions of addicts want to be given a chance...and we get stuck with a shithead like you! We will treat you not because of your fame, money or influence. You are here to be cured, so get cured – or start walking. Am I understood?

"Yes SIR," David replied with a grin after being momentarily stunned. "Has anyone ever told you that you're a real bastard?

"All the time lad," Patla smiled. "Just don't ever forget it, and we'll get along alright."

Dr Meg said that after that her husband was like a "sergeant-major with him. He told him when to take baths, get clean clothes, if he wanted to smoke in the house to ask the hostess's permission, to hold chairs for ladies at the table."

Dr Meg remembers an example of David's new found etiquette. "When we took the family out for an evening he went with us," she remembers. "Patla taught him how to choose what wines to go with what food (his own so-called wealthy and aristocratic family had never bothered, he said, and all he knew about alcohol was beer – and booze to get drunk). Once he had gotten over his anti-social rebellion he was a nice person, and we really enjoyed his company. When we were out one evening I felt a lump in my throat as he fetched my coat and – obviously not quite knowing what he should do to help me, but trying to be polite – he just handed it to me. After six weeks or so he was as normal and acceptable in our home as our own children and ready to go back to the United States."

While away, the two members of the family to whom David was closest, made a fateful decision, at a time when David needed all the help he could find. Bobby Jr and Chris Lawford re-thought their relationship with David while he was in England.

"My cousin David had the gene which runs in our family, that allows incredible abuse to body and mind to little effect," Chris Lawford wrote, "but he was physically frail and his luck wasn't Irish.

"...There was little to look forward to in the late fall of 1978...
"The phone rang," Chris Lawford remembered. "It was Bobby.
RFK JR: Hey man, what's happening?
CHRIS: Nothing, man...What's up?
RFK JR: I'm worried about David. He's getting his ass kicked. We need to help him.
CHRIS: How the hell are we going to do help him, man?
RFK JR: I don't know, but we have to.
CHRIS: We could stop getting high with him.
RFK JR: Maybe that's what we need to do.

"...I knew that if I were to stop getting high with David it would be tantamount to cutting my best friend out of my life," Lawford furthered. "I felt the pain of that, but I was incapable of making another choice. At this point in my life the drugs had become my best friend. My friendship with David would just be another casualty. It's for his own good,' I rationalized. 'He can't handle it. I'm not going to stop using. And if I can't get high with him, the only thing to do is stop hanging out with him. There's no other way.' So once again I ignored what had been in my heart since that day David and I met on the great lawn in Glen Cove, and I said goodbye to my best friend in the world so I could have what I thought I wanted – my drugs and the confidence of the cousin I most admired. The plan didn't work.

Instead of helping my friend, the isolation hastened his slide into the abyss. Later I realized that I never wanted to look at this for what it was. David was becoming the version of me that I did not want to see. The version of me that I never believed was possible. So I turned my back, looked away, and left my best friend to figure it out for himself. I never told David what I decided or why, but I think he knew – and it hurt him."

"After that day I never again had the same relationship with David," Lawford concluded regretfully. "And my pride that Bobby had trusted me felt like what it was: just pride, the worst of the seven deadly sins. It was indeed 'the bitter end.'"

"When David got home, it seemed to us, his problems were insurmountable," Dr. Patterson thought after David's return to the US. "A great deal of David's drug problem lay in his objecting to what the family required in socially 'conforming' in public for appearances' sake..."

The Patterson's kept their promise to David – they went back to the United States with him for discussions with the Kennedys over David's future. The family directed them to Lee Macht, who had been a key figure in putting him in McLeans. They expected problems.

All that David needs," Patla told the psychiatrist, "is a family who cares for him and his real needs, and teaches him basic spiritual values – and kick his backside when he needs it. Someone he trusts and respects."

"Just like that?" Macht asked skeptically. "Do you know how much money he has access to?"

"I thought we were talking about his health, not his wealth," Patla replied bluntly. "But, yes, he has told me, and he is determined to get hold of it and to spend it."

"And you think that's good idea? What do you think will happen if it's all just handed over to him?"

"He would go on a wild spending spree," Patla answered. "He would buy cars, drugs, drink, women – and might die in three months."

"And yet you think it's a good idea?" Macht replied sarcastically.

"Yes I do," Patla affirmed. "Not just because you've tried everything else, legal and illegal, and have failed."

"Why, then, and on what authority?"

"Luke fifteen," Patla said laconically.

Macht pulls open a nearby drawer and opens a Bible.

"Need any help finding it?" Patla suggested dryly.

Macht shook his head and quietly read the Parables of the Lost Sheep, the Lost Coin and the Lost Son.

"It never fails," Patla said firmly. "St. Augustine summed it up well when he said, 'Do as you will, and pay for it.' The secret of course, is not in just suffering the consequences of one's actions, but in the constancy of the father's forgiving love for the prodigal son. For David to be really cured, and not just detoxified, both he and his family would have to read, understand and practice Luke fifteen."

"Otherwise?"

"Otherwise, whatever temporary help we give, he will be back on drugs again within a few weeks or months."

"We met over twenty members of the family at a memorable meeting, Dr. Patterson recalled, "but no David present. David informed me that no-one had spoken to him about the family meeting at all...They said he should keep off drugs, complete his graduation at university, marry a nice girl, and not cause embarrassment to the family. That was all. It looked as if they had never read Luke fifteen!"

Dr. Patterson's lack of sympathy for the family can be forgiven of course. She was not privy to the years of anguish associated with David's addiction and had only a deeply troubled one-sided version of events from which to assess the whole issue. While negative or even sinister motivations have been assigned to the Kennedys desire to keep David's struggles out of the media, the truth is considerably less dramatic. Is it so incredible to want to deal with an addicted loved one privately – especially such a public family like David's? It's very clear to those who are objectively minded, that's David's family have unnecessarily shouldered a lot of the blame for his failings. However you slice it though, Dr. Patterson's treatment had failed. Her claim that David was drug free for "over a year later" was provably inaccurate. David was back at square one. Worse still, he had his sights set on New York City as a permanent base.

12. New York City 1979

After he arrived home from England in early December, and following the family meetings with the Pattersons, David went on a rafting trip with his cousins and other contemporaries for a few weeks over the New Year's period. Following this adventure, he relocated fulltime to New York City in February 1979. Using money from his trust fund, he rented an apartment at East 72nd Street. The official word was that he was there on leave from Harvard and looking for a job. But the reality was that his sole ambition was to party and let his hair down. It was inevitable, considering the fast crowd he was running with, that he would return to his old habits. It became a familiar pattern.

"There were periods where he was fairly clean, off drugs and not drinking a lot," author Harrison Rainie said, "and then periods where he was bingeing."

"David wandered the country aimlessly," a friend said of David's life at the close of the 1970s. "He became a fixture in all-night discos in New York while getting and losing jobs in a week."

Another friend who met him at this time said that he appeared "soft spoken, gentle and would only smile, never laugh. He had the look of someone much older than he was. He liked to sit back and observe the comings and goings of others. None of us ever spoke the thousands of questions we had for him about his family."

"I feel grateful to have had the relationship I had with him," one friend stated to this author. "Grateful that I would meet such a fantastic person. Grateful to have been one that can call him a friend.

"My mom was very ill during some of this," the female friend continued, "and he was so supportive. He would ask about her, and no, he never spoke with her. But you could tell he was genuinely concerned."

"It was tons of fun," said another friend. "David was a real gentleman. He really cared about his friends and treated them well."

Despite his own frequently challenging circumstances, David always reached out to his friends, frequently supporting them in times of crisis. It would be a continuing theme: he was better at helping others than himself.

"It was such an honor for me to meet him," a female friend said to this author, "not because of his name, but, I came to find out very quickly, it was because of his depth and perception...His wisdom and understanding of the people he was in contact with, should have helped him get himself into perspective.

"I know all accounts seem to point differently," the woman furthered, "but the Kennedy family should have been proud to have had David's insight and wisdom, even in the situation he was in."

His friends, while obviously enjoying going along for the ride, worried about him too and reciprocated the help. "He'd come home so completely out of it," said a close friend "you'd have to watch him really carefully. You never knew if he would do something like drop a lighted cigarette and set the place on fire. Everyone around him was completely scared. They were all keeping tabs on him, calling him, calling other people to check where he was and who he was with." This friend recalled staying over at David's apartment one night and woke to see David crying. "I asked him if wanted to talk – he didn't."

One good friend that met David during this time spoke of how he rescued her from a potentially dangerous situation. "I met him at a party in West Palm Beach in Florida," the woman stated to this author in 2009. "He must have been visiting family. He was my knight in shining armor. I was pretty messed up and he saved me from some guys who were messing with me. He asked for my number, saying, 'Someone has to take care of you.' He wanted to know if he could call, was he kidding, of course he could. After we spoke for most of the evening, I went home and so call me a few weeks later, and told me of his family connections...That is what endeared him to me, that and his ability to make me feel at ease in any situation.

"I was not used to someone being like that, in control of a situation without really being controlling," the friend went on. "He was my protector that night, like I said, it was a party, and as parties do, things got rowdy, David must have sensed I needed help."

Lee Macht, David's psychiatrist, had begun to over-prescribe David's medication as a way to keep him off the streets. He was concerned about David's reckless risk taking. Over a 16 month period, Macht wrote 50 prescriptions for Percodan, Dilaudid and Quaaludes – strictly "under the counter." That decision would come back to bite both of them and hard.

A family confidant told the New York Daily News that "David has a lot – and I mean a lot – of emotional problems stemming from the death of his father." One person who tried to help David with his personal issues was his Aunt Jackie – who visited him at least weekly through most of 1979.

Despite the assistance from some of the family, he soon found his old connections again and lost his way back into heroin. His now estranged friendship with Bobby and Chris was still on his mind.

"They'd hang out at Lem's place and never invited me," David lamented, following the split several months prior while he was overseas. "I'd think about what a great time they were having and do heroin by myself."

"I would make the buys of smack while he waited in his car, a BMW, or in a cab," the security guard come dealer said. "He would buy what we call 'bundles' that hold 10 bags with $10 ($30 today) worth of heroin in each bag. I'd say that was a pretty heavy habit."

"I was supplementing the Heroin – five times the lethal dose for someone not used to it – with forty Percodans a day," David said of life in New York. "I'd go up to Boston on the shuttle and get five prescriptions from Lee Macht for forty Percodans each. Then I'd go to various drug stores around town and get them filled and come back to New York with two hundred pills. That was the ritual – once a week."

He still cut a disheveled figure on the streets of New York except on the rare occasions he was required to dress up.

"I remember once when he came to the football banquet where the first Robert Kennedy awards were being given out," said a female acquaintance, "and you could see his mother's face light up because she was so surprised and pleased to see he'd put on a tie and jacket."

"He always looked like he just got out of bed," a male friend stated. "He was always wearing a rumpled white shirt and a pair of jeans." Even in the discos of Manhattan his attire remained unchanged.

"I thought it was kind of endearing," a woman who accompanied him said. "It made me think he was very unpretentious."

One short-lived romance, typical of the kind he had experienced in the preceding few years, was with a Connecticut woman, Ryan Rayston.

"He turned me onto drugs," she claimed, "and took me on a drug-buying binge in South America. I was a student at Dartmouth College and we used to go skiing together. I also saw him in Palm Beach. Despite his drug addiction, David was a darling, very gentle, extremely sweet, not like the other members of the clan."

"David loved beautiful women," a friend said, "and dated Cheryl Tiegs and Robert Redford's daughter, Shauna, as well as Rachel Ward. But he was so addicted to drugs and alcohol and self-destruction, he was incapable of forming a relationship."

"David had a cutting wit...and often tried to be a clown, but his pranks just weren't funny. He thought that his jokes were in the Kennedy tradition of fun-loving mischief, but they tended to be mean and a cruel parody of the Kennedy humor...but David was seldom interested in talking about anything but girls and drugs," the friend furthered.

Although there had been numerous flings in the five years since his relationship with Pam Kelley, there hadn't any serious, all-consuming involvements. But that was about to change.

There's some debate as when and how David met starlet Rachel Ward. One line of thinking is that they met on a South American rafting trip at the very end of 1978 after David returned from England. They almost certainly met through Bobby jr and his girlfriend at the time, Rebecca Frazer. She was the daughter of prominent British politician Sir Hugh Frazer and moved in similar circles to Rachel.

Regardless, by the time spring arrived they were dating. While it was intense and passionate, unfortunately, it wasn't to last – before the year was out, the media was already talking about them in the past tense.

Rachel represented something special to David – his version of the perfect partner. In his words, "the most beautiful woman who ever lived." She had the physical appearance that David tended to be attracted to: tall (5'9"), busty, brunette with captivating dark eyes and a statuesque, almost aristocratic bearing. A rebellious attitude against their privileged upbringing and a shared unpretentiousness brought them into the same orbit. She was also very bright and shared David's sense of fun and off-beat humor.

"We had good times," David later recalled. "She was just really getting into her acting career..." Rachel later commented that the attraction was mutual.

"He was crazy, with a wonderful sense of humor, and he was always very merry," she said. "He talked about Teddy and his father and his family in a happy way." Although Rachel added that she thought the comparisons were uncomfortable for him.

His sloppiness was still evident, as was his lack of attention to his diet. "He ate like a pig and didn't take very good care of himself," Rachel asserted. She denied ever knowing about his hard drug use. "We smoked joints now and then," she said, "but there was no suggestion of heroin."

David backed this up. "Rachel wanted to get an apartment with me and settle down. But I knew I was too fucked up. I was back on smack. She had no idea of what I was up to. I don't know what she thought of all those little marks on my arms when I was naked. I guess she thought they were some odd Kennedy rash. We never talked about it."

Early in their relationship David got very jealous when, one night at Xenon, French playboy Phillipe Junot decided to pay Rachel a little too much attention. He knocked Junot's arm off of Rachel's shoulder, which caused the Frenchman to leap to feet. David ended on the floor with a broken nose. It was duly noted in the Chatterbox section of People magazine in early March.

If David appeared upset by the attention Rachel was getting, he was considerably more at ease when the roles were reversed.

"Lots of good-looking women were always hanging around him," said a person who frequented the clubs at this time. "Press agents would push their clients up to him and say, 'Here, dance with this guy.' And the next day this or that girl's picture would be in the paper. I'm not saying he wasn't nice, but he was a kid. That was a childish thing to do, that thing with Phillipe Junot, the kind of thing a high school boy does when someone cuts in on his date. In that crowd it was ridiculous."

More drama arose from his recklessness and impulsiveness. Apart from yet another traffic violation (for not having a license), he broke his left leg playing "touch" football with his brothers. On April 29, 1979, his first stop after being released from hospital was his favorite nightclub – Xenon. He would be pictured – leg cast and all – dancing the night away with a bevy of beauties.

But the relationship with Rachel continued. "I remember once we went to see The Invasion of the Body Snatchers," David said, "and at one point in the movie she let out this blood curdling scream. 'Practicing?' I asked her. Then at another scary moment I let out my own scream, and some guys in front of us told me to shut up." Then as quickly as the relationship started, it was finished.

When he wasn't tearing up the dance floors of the Manhattan discos, he would concentrate on writing projects on people who were of interest to him. They seem to have been out of personal enjoyment rather than for professional recognition, as none have yet come to light. One subject he was researching during his New York period was the influential African-

Behind Blue Eyes

American lawyer and businessman Vernon Jordan Jr (1935-), who at the time headed the civil rights organization National Urban League. Unfortunately, David's project remained unfinished. While his talent and brain-power was never in question, his life was not conducive to the disciplined thinking needed to get a writing career off the ground.

During the summer David stayed at a friend's house in Boston. He had just arrived from Maine where he had bought a green-colored BMW sports coupe. He got clocked doing more than 100 miles (160 km) per hour on the Maine Turnpike. The friend asked what happened next.

"They let me go," David replied.
"They shouldn't have," was the reply.
"They always do," he said.

A few days later, the friend found drug paraphernalia in the bedside drawer David was using.
"I'm sorry," David answered when he was confronted.
"You know what you are?" he was asked.
"I know," he answered. "I'm a junkie."
"You've got that exactly right," he was told.
"I can't help it," he had said then. "I'd like to stop. I really would. I just can't help it."

Later that day, the friend saw David sitting in his living room. He was transfixed on a photo of his father sitting on an end table next to the couch. The friend recalled how moving a scene it was – father and son sharing a private, much needed moment together.

That night, David left the house voluntarily. He wrote a note to the host saying that it was never his intention to embarrass anyone or have anybody feel awkward or obligated to allow him to stay on. He apologized for his weakness and held out the hope that he could eventually exercise the demon within.

There was a touching moment that same summer on the Cape. Over a few days, David befriended a 7 year old girl who was afraid of the water. He spent hours with her teaching her how to swim and to overcome her fear. Less than five year later, when David passed away, the girl remembered her time with David during the summer of '79. She rang her dad at his work.

"Daddy, did you hear? David is dead" she said.
"I know," her father said softly.
"Oh Daddy, it's so sad. He was so nice."

Back in New York at the end of summer, life was about to throw David yet another curve ball – this one with life altering consequences.

13. Harlem Bust and Intervention

On Wednesday, September 5, David noticed he was becoming unwell, and realized he'd been infected with endocarditis again. He rang Lee Macht to arrange treatment at Massachusetts General Hospital. But before heading to Boston, David decided to make a final drug buy. This time he would not rely on his middle man. It proved a fateful decision.

David and an unidentified friend from Connecticut were driving in David's recently purchased BMW sports car on West 116th Street at around 5:15 p.m., when two men waved down the vehicle. After parking the $16,000 ($50,000 today) Beemer, David said he was forced at knifepoint into the seedy Shelton Plaza and robbed of $30 and beaten up. But nobody was fooled. 25 glassine envelopes of heroin were found on the hotel landing.

An emergency call came through a 5:29 p.m. from a woman who told the 911 operator that a "white fellow is hemmed up and he's full of blood." The friend from Connecticut then made a call that was registered at 5:42 p.m. "I came down from Connecticut with a friend of mine," he told the operator. "He's in the Shelton Hotel and they've got a knife around his neck and they're trying to stick him up." Police arrived soon afterwards and found David dazed and disorientated, dressed in a sports jacket, dress shirt and trousers.

"With the wheels, he was easy to spot," said a narcotics division source, in reference to David's BMW. "He ran into trouble last night because his usual tout wasn't out front, but somebody knew he had bread and figured he was a mark..."

"I should have just said it was no big deal and walked off," David later remarked. "But I was so out of it that I walked up to the cop in charge and started acting suspicious and said I didn't want to get involved. Naturally I was arrested and the next day the news was all over the papers. David fucks up again."

David was never actually arrested as the police turned up before any drug transaction took place and he was therefore listed as a victim. A search of the vehicle turned up four unpaid parking fines and the Beemer he was driving had expired Virginia plates.

The question the media was asking was the same one asked by the Shelton Plaza day manager Cassandra Brown. "This boy has all the money in the world. Why should he come up here?" His six-year secret life was exposed.

He was taken from the 28th Precinct in Harlem to the 24th Precinct station on West 100th Street where he was interviewed for a couple of hours.

"Please this can't get into the papers," David told the officers, "I just want to catch a plane to Hyannis." He was asked about his presence in such a seedy location. "I was just riding through when two guys beckoned me with their hands," David answered. "I just wanted to see what they wanted." He was then driven home to his East Side apartment by the friend from Connecticut. A police narcotics source says David was badly shaken by the evening's events. "He was really shaken up," the officer stated. "He was plain scared. He hands were shaking and he was near tears."

Steve Smith arrived the next day to take David back to Hyannis Port. "He was ordered to the family compound so that he could be watched closely," an insider revealed. "Everyone is deeply concerned."

A couple of days after the Harlem incident the newspapers were telling the world that David had run away – given the family the slip. But it was a short lived escape – 36 hours in fact. The next news of him came through shortly afterwards – he was in hospital. He had admitted himself in a very serious condition with endocarditis to a Boston hospital on Sunday, September 9th. They transferred him to Massachusetts General, later the same day for more specialized treatment.

David's Uncle Steve Smith's much mocked statement that David was "suffering from an ailment similar to drug addiction" failed to highlight the genuine worry that the family had for David's welfare.

"The family has for a long time been much concerned about his condition," Steve Smith said in the statement, "and has endeavored and will continue to endeavor to help him in what is finally a long and hard personal as well as medical struggle."

"He is physically sick and receiving medical care," Bobby Jr said when contacted about his younger brother's condition. But in the next breath, an unguarded moment, he showed the depth of his concern. "I'm shocked by all this," RFK jr added. "It's a big family – people take different paths. But David is very bright and really, really sensitive."

According to a family insider, David ignored the family's sentiments. "Since the Harlem incident, everyone has been trying to help him, but he has indicated a strong desire to be left alone," the person said. He had agreed though to sign a 6 month guardianship on October 15th while still in the hospital.

While stoic in public, the emotional impact on David's immediate family was privately taking its toll. "I toss and turn all night thinking what would Bobby do?" Ted said, in a candid moment to an aide. "...And I swear to Christ, I don't have a clue what Bobby would do. And I think, Jesus Christ, if Bobby were alive, none of this would be happening."

"Look, don't beat yourself up over this thing," the aide replied. "You're doing what you can."

"But I promised I would I would be there for these kids," Ted said in obvious distress. "I promised Ethie. I feel like I'm letting her down."

Just then, Ethel entered the room and stood in front of the Senator from Massachusetts, hands on hips. "I never want to hear you say that, Ted Kennedy. I never want to hear you say you are letting me or Bobby down. Because it's not the truth. It's not the truth Teddy."

Ted looked up at her and nodded.

"These bad things happen to so many people in the world in which we live," said a Kennedy family friend. "David has had to live it all in the newspapers. When I saw him right after all the publicity about the Harlem thing, he said to me, 'That guy in all those stories isn't me. I don't know who they're talking about."

As the stories continued to analyze why David had strayed from his path, his friends were angered that the personality of the man they knew and loved was being ignored. Some refused to discuss him at all.

"He needs to know he can trust me not to provide more grist for the mill at this tough time," one friend said.

Others, on the promise of anonymity, described him as a bright, funny, sensitive and energetic young man. "The kind of guy who'd go dancing with a broken leg, the kind of guy almost anyone would want as a friend."

Meanwhile, back at Massachusetts General, David was developing a reputation for being a difficult patient. His frustration and unhappiness at his seven-week confinement were taking its toll. He would frequently throw things at nurses and other patients in his vicinity. But at least he was slowly rallying.

He was put on methadone as a detox measure. Rachel Ward visited regularly, supposedly his only visitor. They made loved, but both understood that David needed to get himself right. There couldn't be a future – they were being pulled in different directions. David would hold a candle for Rachel for the rest of his life.

As his health improved, he wandered through the hospital. A young woman with terminal cancer was one that he met. He had a friend smuggle him in a bottle of champagne which he and the girl drank while they made love. He was discharged from the hospital on October 25th, under the very watchful eye of his family.

David had hit rock bottom – there could be no going back. "I think we should have an intervention," Joan suggested to several family members at a meeting regarding David.

"Well, I think that's just a marvelous idea," Eunice thought. "I am totally convinced of its viability as a solution."

Her husband Sargent Shriver had reservations. He thought that it might appear to David that everyone was ganging up on him. "That will just piss him off, then what?"

"It has to be Ethie's decision," Ted announced. "Let's run it by her and see what she thinks. I agree with Joansie, though, we have to do something. And I like the idea."

Ethel shared Sarge's concerns, but admitted to being at the end of her rope. She decided that yes, an intervention was the way forward, but would not be present when David was confronted.

"I got pulled into the aftermath," Richard Burke commented, "coordinating discussions with the family to set up treatment for David. I worked with Steve Smith and several physicians and counselors...One suggestion was that we find David a sponsor, someone who could pal around with him and serve as a combination friend/confidant/policeman. In essence, a guardian to protect David from himself.

"Along with David's older brother Joe," Burke continued, "I planned the details of an intervention (at a nearby hotel) wherein David's family confronted him with his problem..."

"To my memory," Burke continued, "all of his brothers and sisters were present. We had a psychiatrist there who acted as a mediator. We had a facility lined up and the plan was to take David right over there from the hotel. They all told David how much they loved him and how disappointed in him they all were, and that if he didn't straighten up his act they were going to stop communicating with him. It was standard intervention material. Very tough. Very upsetting. Lots of tears. I recall that when someone brought up that his uncle Teddy was disappointed in him, David really lashed out. 'The way he drinks, and the way he treats Aunt Joan?' David thundered. How does he get off being disappointed in me?

"I am always being chewed out by my uncle," David said, "and I feel really bad about it. The whole thing is messed up."

Another said to have poured out words of tenderness to David was his older brother Bobby. "We love you," he told David. "But you're killing yourself and it's killing us to see you doing this to yourself."

The hypocrisy of Bobby's statement, himself a heroin addict at the time, infuriated David, who angrily replied: "You ought to know!"

"To be honest I don't think it did any good," Richard Burke refelcted. "I'm not sure we understood the depth of his shame that the guilt he felt about the relapses was partly responsible for his wanting to continue to medicate himself, if you will. He was so ashamed, and he kept saying as much. Even with the shrink there, I just had the feeling we were in over our heads with this thing. He absolutely refused to go to the facility, and short of dragging him over there, what could we do? The next day, I reported back to the senator that I didn't think the intervention had been successful. He was crestfallen. 'Goddamn!' he told me. 'I don't know why, but I just thought it would work. I really did.'"

David's now very public problems became Lee Macht's also. Police in Harlem had discovered Macht's prescriptions in the glove box of David's Beemer amongst the unpaid parking fines. He was fined $1,000 and stripped of his license to prescribe stronger, restricted meds, but still allowed to practice medicine.

David had cheated death – yet again – just. "He is an awfully nice guy," said Xenon friend, Madeleine Fudeman. "Maybe it's better he got caught now, before he is too far gone."

While the mire of Roxbury was a harrowing and embarrassing event for David, he was able to close a lengthy chapter in his life. A new, quieter, happier life was born out of the ashes – Sacramento beckoned.

Behind Blue Eyes

PART 4: REGAINING HIS BALANCE: SACRAMENTO YEARS
1980 - 1982

15. Living in Exile: Don Juhl 1980

By the time David Kennedy left Sacramento in September 1982, his view of the Californian capital was very different from the one he held on his arrival, two-and-a-half years earlier. Though he grew to love his time in the river city, when he landed with his drug counselor, Don Juhl during the first week of February 1980, he felt as if he were in exile from his family. It had been a tumultuous few months.

The late 70s saw David at his lowest ebb. Following his premature departure from Harvard, his use of drugs had escalated alarmingly. There were o.d.'s and hospitalizations for both drug and non-drug related illnesses. There were also minor skirmishes with the law for traffic offences, to say nothing of the turmoil his addictions had on his personal relationships, family especially. Much to David's embarrassment, most of his transgressions were duly noted in the press. However, despite this, he managed to keep his clandestine use of narcotics under wraps from the rest of the world, until an ill-advised trip to Harlem in New York on September 5th, 1979,

Driving his newly purchased tan BMW sports coupe to 1116th Street near Eighth Avenue, David headed to the Shelton Plaza Hotel in Harlem. It was 5:30 p.m. on a steamy New York afternoon when David and a male friend from Connecticut decided to make a heroin buy. The hotel was a known shooting gallery and residents stated that they had seen David there many times before. This time however, he found trouble instead of his connection.

David told police he was flagged down by two men near the hotel and forced at knifepoint into the lobby. He was beaten and robbed of $30, although police say he may have been carrying as much as $500. No arrests were made as police turned up before any drug transaction took place. However, the secret life David had been able to conceal became embarrassingly public.

Becoming seriously ill with endocarditis again, David voluntarily checked himself into a Boston hospital where a full seven-week stay ensued. He condition was listed as very serious - he came close to death.

"He was a very, very sick man," one close family friend said. "He almost didn't make it... the drugs almost got him." The friend says that his options had run out. "His alternative was further degradation and death in a few short months...I think that was the thing that made up his mind (to get help). He knew that he was not far from an ignominious and frightful death."

While recuperating in the hospital, the family had David sign a 6-month guardianship on October 15th, 1979. David was suspicious of their true motivations. "I told them from an objective point of view I found it rather interesting that the only time anybody ever gave a damn was when I fucked up," he said. "...When they finally did do something, it seemed like it was more to keep me from o.d.'ing in the street and causing a problem for Teddy's campaign than anything else."

David said he felt betrayed by the family and thought they were conspiring against him. At his sister Courtney's wedding in June of 1980, David felt everyone's eyes staring at him. He turned to his Aunt Joan and said, "They're all looking at the junkie. That's what I am to them...I'm sorry I'm so weak. I just don't want you or anyone else I love to lose faith in me. I feel I'm not good enough to be a Kennedy. All I've done in recent years is bring shame on my family." If anyone knew how David felt it was Ted's first wife. David seemed to have benefited from their lengthy chat.

"David didn't think the family really wanted to help him," a friend recalled. "Just keep him out of the way so any scandal involving him would be kept quiet and not tarnish Ted's presidential chances." The friend thought David saw himself as the scapegoat, feeling picked on by his family.

The family gave him 2 options: back to the psychiatric wing of McLeans, in Boston, or head out to Sacramento in California for one-on-one treatment. "Naturally, I chose the latter," David commented wryly. Enter Don Juhl.

Donald Juhl was a 41 year old bearded, street-smart drug counselor and head of a rehabilitation centre called Aquarian Effort, when he came into David's life in November of 1979. A friend said that he "looks like a cowboy and talks like a cowboy but is wise in the ways of the streets." A Democratic state official in California recommended him to Steve Smith after his own son had received treatment. After checking Juhl's credentials with both East and West Coast medical experts, Smith hired him to treat David at the so called "Kennedy compound" in Hyannis Port. The family requested privacy, but the identity of his patient was soon leaked out after Juhl had to explain his continuing absence to the board members of Aquarian Effort.

Something of a celebrity detoxifier, his treatment program in 1980 cost $20,000 per month ($60,000 today) which came out of David's trust fund. That was his Uncle Ted's idea, something that left David privately fuming. He felt Juhl was overrated and ridiculously overpriced.

"I agreed to take it because my Uncle Ted told me to get my act together or I'd wind up in an institution for the rest of my life like his sister Rosemary," David told a friend. "If my father was alive," David said at another time, "he'd never have sent me here."

Juhl's method for rehabilitation involved intense one-on-one around the clock supervision. David would not be allowed out of his sight. Juhl was even present for the family's annual end of year skiing vacation at Aspen, Colorado. David described the methods as "therapy by humiliation." David said when he appeared one morning in a long sleeve shirt on a warm day he was asked rather sharply, "What's the matter David? Are you afraid to roll up your sleeves and show us your tracks?"

Until David's guardianship ended on April 15th, 1980, he would stay with Juhl and his wife in their duplex. Cousin Chris Lawford says, "David chose Sacramento...primarily to get as far away from the family as he could. He spent that year in his room in Sacramento watching Uncle Teddy's campaign unravel on his black and white TV...He wasn't toasting anyone and nobody was toasting him."

David emerged for his only public appearance with Don Juhl on March 15th. The papers reported that David had made the unexpected visit to a local high school as part of Ted's presidential bid. More unexpectedly, he gave the convention speech – impressing everyone with his eloquence and presentation. But Teddy failed to gain the student's nomination.

The newspaper duly reported the event titled "Effort in Vain."

"Sacramento, Calif (AP). David Kennedy, in a rare public appearance since beginning drugs counseling, stumped for his uncle Edward M. Kennedy at a high school convention, but the Massachusetts Senator lost the student vote.

Kennedy, 24, son of the late Robert F. Kennedy, on Saturday, attended a presidential nominating convention of the California Junior Statesmen of America, composed of high school students.

He made the nomination speech for his uncle, who is seeking the Democratic nomination for President, stressing that, "My uncle believes the government must intervene and establish wage and price controls."

But President Carter won with 171, Kennedy had 96. Kennedy told reporters he had been staying with his drug counselor Donald Juhl in Sacramento for several weeks...Kennedy and Juhl refused to answer questions about drugs, but Juhl said, "Everything is just fine."

Perhaps not. Privately, David told friends he was becoming increasingly dissatisfied with Juhl's methods and the exorbitant cost. "Juhl told me there were three rules," David said later. "I had to jog every day, I wasn't allowed to say 'Fuck off and die' anymore. And no drugs. If I broke any of these rules it would cost me another month, and every month I was there cost me $20,000 of my own money."

It came as no surprise that David voluntarily left Juhl when he was legally able to in mid April of 1980. However, during a short visit to New York the previous month, he told friends there that he would stay on in Sacramento rather than return back east. It was simple he told a journalist. "The people are friendly, the weather is nice and it's well located." And people didn't make a fuss over him. He was able to escape the glare of the public eye, something he loathed.

A girlfriend that came into David's life during his first months in Sacramento was Nancy Narleski. The 19 year-old brunette was a local girl working on Teddy's presidential campaign in the early spring when she met David. Despite her support of Teddy's election ambitions, she didn't endear herself to the family. She was quite prepared to tell them what she regarded as their short-comings where David was concerned. She would later make the allegations that both Teddy and Kennedy cousin Willy Smith had propositioned her. When Smith was charged with rape in 1991, Narleski came forward to say that Smith had made the sexual advances towards her in a hotel room during the 1980 campaign. When later told of the incident, David appeared unconcerned and rather unsympathetic, saying that she should have known what they were like. After their brief time together they picked up again shortly before his death. She believed the family didn't do enough to help David, whom she thought was misunderstood. She added perceptively: "The Kennedys were David's real addiction."

Some think he bummed around for the duration of his stay in Sacramento, but really he was re-learning how to function with some semblance of normality. Outward signs of progress may not have been too forthcoming, but internally, and emotionally, he was regaining his balance. In Sacramento, he was able to learn how to put one foot in front of the other largely on his own terms, far away from prying eyes and Kennedys.

David was "agonizing over a new direction for his life" and that he was "yearning to get back into the mainstream," he told a friend. But first he needed to find his own place.

He found his new digs and took a lease out on a small midtown apartment at 24th and Q streets. After a break in left him without his expensive stereo equipment, he moved into a single bedroom apartment in North Sacramento.

After intense media and family pressure for the previous eight months, the first stage of his new life was understandably difficult. He felt as if he were a tight-rope walker without a net.

"I began to concentrate on having a mental breakdown," David said of this time. However, he soon made new friends who were drawn to his quiet, gentle spirit. These new contacts didn't appear to be star struck by the Kennedy name and appreciated David's qualities and celebrated his unique character. This aided David's recovery and gave him a much needed sense of stability, that safety net he felt was missing when he first ventured out on his own.

He soon adapted to the laid back, outdoor Californian lifestyle. He snow-skied during the winter months, and water skied in the summer. He also swam, jogged, played tennis and tossed a football. He even attended classes at the University of California in Davis when the mood struck him. He reveled in his anonymity on the West Coast. He felt he could cultivate his own talents, but still become the man he needed to be in order to function within the parameters set down by his family.

One of his new friends was 34 year-old Dave Kelley, manager of one of David's favorite hang-outs, Harry's Bar and Grill. Kelley thought David to be shy, quiet, painfully private and seemingly troubled. But added, "Everybody liked him."

"He was always a real nice, quiet guy," says Limelight Café owner, Danny Payne. "He once even tried to sell me some Amway products."

"He had a lot of friends," says Randy Paragary, a lawyer who owned the Lord Beaverbrook and Harry's Bar and Grill. "Most of them were sincere. They weren't Kennedy groupies. No one was really that impressed with him. And I think that's why he liked Sacramento so much. He felt more at ease, more relaxed than at home where the press was always around. He didn't go for the celebrity thing. He didn't hide the fact he was a Kennedy. But he'd feel uncomfortable if anyone would introduce him as 'David Kennedy, Robert Kennedy's son.' I thought he had a lot going for him. Especially since he planned to go back to school and follow a career in law. I would think he had a bright future. He had a real good sense of humor. He laughed a lot."

"He did seem to be drawn to those who appreciated him for his individuality and not his name," one friend told this author in 2009. "Although he loved his family, he did not like the star-struck quality that being a Kennedy caused. He wanted to be a friend for just a friend, and not because one felt privileged to know him because his last name happened to be Kennedy.

"It was in those candid moments," the friend furthered, "I was able to at least get a glimpse of him and how he may have turned out had things been different. I feel sure that he would have raised his children with an abiding respect for family and country while showing them the real Kennedy legacy, not the fake one. He would have been honest and upfront with them, as he was with his friends."

Sacramento advertising consultant, Patrick Powers was an acquaintance of David's also. He saw David regularly let his hair down at local nightspots. "I saw him party and I saw him get stoned," he said. "He never really got off it."

One of the more significant friendships to enter David's life was 35 year-old Nancie Alexander, whom he met in June 1980. She was a hair-stylist and had contacts with Juhl's Aquarian Effort. He couldn't have met someone more diametrically opposite to himself. On the surface it seemed an unlikely pairing. She was ten years his senior, a conservative republican, and a fundamentalist Christian. Though strictly plutonic, their friendship during David's time at Sacramento blossomed. David found a confidant in the maternal Nancie.

"I said to him, 'Do you think that people expect more of you because of who you are?' He said, 'People should expect more. I have everything they want and they don't understand why I don't use it to the fullest.'"

Another important event occurred for David in June 1980 – he turned 25. Attainment of this milestone meant he came into his inheritance. At his death a dozen years earlier, RFK's estate was worth an estimated $12 million ($75 million today). This was divided into two parts: half to be distributed among his 11 offspring and the remaining half to his widow, Ethel. Heavy family expenses over the years had whittled this down considerably. Even so, with Juhl's expenses taken into consideration, David's share came to about $430,000 ($1.2 million today). However, it was tied up in family trust funds and he was unable to access the full amount. He was able to get his hands on the interest, which afforded him an allowance of around $35,000 per year ($90,000 today). While not a fortune, it was still a very comfortable salary for a young single man at the time. The US national average in 1980 was $24,000 for a 4 person family – but it wasn't comfortable enough for David.

"Bobby Kennedy's children are always complaining about not having enough money to live on," a family friend stated.

"They are the poor folks of the Kennedy clan," thought author and journalist Harrison Rainie.

"Ethel paid some of David's expenses, like his drug treatments and the cost of his plane flights," one close family source revealed. "But she regularly refused his requests for additional money."

Contrary to the belief that no family members visited him, David's mother Ethel, did in fact see him on several occasions. "She's just doing her motherly thing," he'd tell his friends. A shroud of secrecy always enveloped the trips, usually on the pretense of social visits to San Francisco or nearby Davis. Nancie Alexander said David would be left depressed after each visit.

"David desperately wanted his mother to be involved in his life," she asserted. "But it was clear to him that she was not going to be...David wanted his mother's respect, he wanted to grow up and he wanted to be well."

"My mother's not involved in anybody's life except her own," David angrily told Nancie Alexander after one of Ethel's flying visits. "We have a whole slew of people raising us and she's not one of them. My mother loves to be busy. Just look at People magazine and you'll see her playing tennis and skiing. But she's not around for us.

"She's oblivious to my problems," David continued. "She doesn't love me. She never wanted 11 children. It was my father who wanted all those kids. It was part of his Kennedy dynasty concept. My father felt that Uncle Ted and John didn't do their part, so my father made up for it."

David's growing resentment of his perceived treatment from the family was further exacerbated one day during the summer of 1980. Reading a copy of *High Times* magazine on the banks of the Sacramento River and over wine with friends, David read an article on his Aunt Rosemary, with whom he identified strongly. Born with a minor intellectual disability, her father, David's grandfather, Joe Kennedy, had her lobotomized from which she was left profoundly incapacitated. She was hurried off to a nursing home in Wisconsin where she remained until her death in 2005, aged 86. She hadn't spoken a word since her operation in 1940, 65 years earlier.

In the article David said his Aunt "had a new pair of white shoes on and was smiling. The thought crossed my mind that if my grandfather was alive, the same thing could have happened to me that happened to her. She was an embarrassment; I am an embarrassment. She was a hindrance; I am a hindrance. As I looked at this picture, I began to hate my grandfather and all of them for having done the thing they had done to her and for doing the thing they were doing to me."

Perhaps because of his isolation from his family, David seemed to develop a need to have contact with his past. He reached out to his first girlfriend Pam Kelley. David wanted Pam to fly out to California and visit him. She agreed to the trip, with David telling her to "leave your wheelchair there." Pam told David that was impossible. "I can't leave my wheelchair here David," she answered. "It's part of me and I'm part of it."

Just when his life seemed to be settling down again, another round of unwanted publicity emerged, causing David more embarrassment. Shortly after midnight Sunday July 28th, 1980, David was pulled over by the Sacramento police for driving the wrong way on a downtown street and going through a stop sign. Police said that he failed a roadside sobriety test and had a blood alcohol level of 0.17% when tested at police headquarters a little later on. He was subsequently booked at the county jail for driving while intoxicated and not being in possession of a valid license.

Don Juhl when contacted about the incident played down its significance. "As far the problems of the past go, they're all over. He's is no kind of trouble," the detoxer concluded. "David's problem has never been drinking and it's certainly not his problem now. It was just less than wise judgment to drive after drinking anything."

David didn't wait around for the fall out. He immediately decided to hitch-hike across the country to the east coast and visit family. His next known whereabouts are in High Point, North Carolina on Friday, August 1, five days after his latest brush with the law. He meets a young local woman in the restaurant where she was waitressing. Speaking of her weekend fling with David for the first time in a 2009 interview with the author of this book, the woman spoke candidly about her brief association with RFK's third son.

"My meeting with David was something like *The Bridges of Madison County* movie," she said. "I had just moved back to High Point, NC...I was separated from my husband at the time, and working as a waitress at a local steak house in High Point. The restaurant was right beside a Motel 6 right off the I-85 interstate highway. I waited on him in the restaurant one Friday night, and he invited me to have a beer in the lounge after I got off work that night. Our Friday night drink turned into a weekend of smoking pot and going to a concert in Darlington, S.C.

"When David left out the following Monday morning, taking off to the I-85 and sticking out his thumb, before he left, I met him in his motel room, and gave him a royal goodbye. He promised me he would call – blah blah blah. It was sort of sad, kind of like the ending of *The Last of the Mohicans*.

"He did indeed call me several months later," the woman volunteered. "But my circumstances had changed and my husband was there with me when he called. I pretended that I did not know him, that he had a wrong number. Such drama!

"When I first met David," the woman continued, "he told me just to call him California, and then he said that his name was Sterling. It wasn't until the last few moments we were together that he told me that his real name was David. He said that his family was very wealthy, and a famous American family.

"He intimated that he had been the black sheep or the proverbial fuck-up in his family. And looking back now, I know he had to be struggling with drug addiction, but I had never really been around a real drug addict, and I didn't recognize all the signs staring me in the face. Since then, I have often wondered how my life would have turned out if I had accepted his phone calls."

Back in Sacramento on August 25th, David's lawyer entered a plea of not guilty in front of municipal court judge Lorenzo Patino, who scheduled a pre-trial conference for October 3rd. David later changed his plea to guilty. He didn't need to appear in court, and through his lawyer, paid the mandatory $380 fine for a first drink driving offence. The charge of un-licensed driving was dropped. Thankfully for David, it would be his last public misdemeanor as he subsequently laid low and settled into something resembling normality.

16. Life in the River City

While leisure activities took precedence during his time in Sacramento, he obtained employment for brief periods also. This was largely out of necessity as he was forever short of money despite his good income (This didn't stop David from writing a $500 rubber check for a complete service on his BMW!) His first job was with the State Lands Commission in 1980 through Kennedy family friend and state controller Ken Cory. At the interview Cory asked David "Are you prepared to go all out and bust your butt?" David replied "No I'm not." Much to David's surprise, he got the job after Frank Gifford, whose daughter Vicki was marrying Michael Kennedy, heard about the incident and intervened. Gifford called Cory and asked him to hire David.

The following year he hooked up with Amway and in the words of Nancie Alexander, enthusiastically "believed he could become a millionaire." But when the millions didn't quite roll in as planned, he settled for a 3 month long, $500 a week ($1300 today) construction job. The company, Ticon Pacific, specialized in pre-cast concreting and worked out of West Sacramento. This job was obtained for him through contractor Mike Heller, a friend of Ethel Kennedy. He finished up there just before he left Sacramento.

Nancie Alexander says David's professional direction left a lot to be desired. "If you were around David for any time, it would make you cry," she said. "He was so lost. He was bent on going down a one way street the wrong way."

He happily remained out of the public eye for most of 1981, except for an appearance at that year's annual RFK Tennis Tournament, much to the delight of the photographers – who kept their lenses trained on him.

But there were important developments in his life away from the preying eyes of the media. Arguably the most significant woman entered his life during the late summer of 1981. She was Paula Scully, a tall, New York based brunette, born in the same year as David. She was a freelance fashion photographer when she met David at Hickory Hill when visiting a friend who was staying at the RFK family home. They hit it off immediately and Paula relocated to Sacramento and moved into David's North Area pad.

"When Paula came into his life they were inseparable," Alexander said. "She accepted him 100% and she took care of him. Paula wasn't into drugs." She insisted David not use drugs in her presence, an edict with which he completely complied.

David first love Pam Kelley agrees. "She cared a lot for David. And she made him behave himself." The Kennedy family liked Paula and there was even talk they had suggested marriage to David. Though they eventually ended their romantic relationship, they would remain close friends until David's death.

"Paula was not taken in by the 'Kennedy mystique' stuff,'" said a friend who saw her around David a great deal. "She saw something in David that she loved and she hung with him during some pretty brutal times. I think that was why David was so taken by her. No one had ever stuck it out with him through the worst times and she was always there. It was very touching to him and an important part of whatever satisfaction he got out of life."

There were plenty of good times too. They frequented night clubs and were snapped dancing away into the wee hours. "He was witty, amusing, intellectual, vibrant, and a bundle of joy to be with," Paula said. "He loved dancing and so do I. It was a lot of fun to be with him."

Nancie Alexander says she became aware of a dangerous game David began playing. He would deliberately put himself into a hypoglycemic-like condition by subsisting on only cheese slices and Pepsi, while drinking heavily.

"Because he couldn't get any drugs into his system, he allowed this to happen," Alexander said. "It altered his state of consciousness – and that was David's goal. I found out about his hypoglycemic game one day when I went over to his apartment. Paula, who was very, very good to David and took care of him, was really angry and was saying, 'You do this on purpose. This is stupid. It's dangerous.' He laughed and said, 'I'm not diabetic. I'm only hypoglycemic.' Paula was furious and told him, 'It's still a deadly game."

"I thought I was in the Mafia," David said of these experiences. "I thought I was the Supreme Ultimate Shibumi Assassin. I thought I was Lee Harvey Oswald. I thought I killed my father. Then I thought my father was trying to drown me in the surf at Malibu." When Nancy Narleski visited him one time, he told her that he thought his Uncle Teddy was behind the recent death of Al Lowenstein and that he would kill again if not stopped.

Narleski became concerned enough for David that at times she thought he might even die. During the late spring of 1980, lifelong Kennedy friend Barbara Kirby received a panicked call from Narleski. Kirby immediately called David's eldest brother Joe telling him of the desperate plight. Joe rang Narleski and exploded, "Don't you call the Kirby's! Everything is under control! There are a lot of things you don't understand. This is the big leagues, so just butt out! Just forget that David Kennedy exists!" Narleski asked Joe if he was threatening her. He responded, "You can take what I've said any way you want to," and slammed down the receiver.

A third Nancy entered his life during this period. 33 year-old cocktail waitress Nancy Esparza said she and David would regularly get together. During the day they'd sunbathe at

David's favorite beaches and hit the bars at night. Esparza says David was free of hard drugs.

"He was somewhat misguided," she said. "He had no sense of direction because of his past circumstances. Though he was bothered by his name, he sometimes used it to get things he wanted. He was a nice guy, a crazy guy, a little off like all of us."

Meanwhile, David's siblings and cousins were starting to fly the coop. marriages were taking place on average of one per year, all of which David attended. While he enjoyed the festivities, the hypocrisy behind Bobby Jr's was almost too much for him to withstand.

In April 1982, RFK Jr married attractive lawyer Emily Black in the bride's home state of Indiana in the society wedding of the year.

"I remember he called me right after Bobby married Emily," former Nashville girlfriend Claire recalled for this author. "David thought it was another strike against him. The perfect Teflon Bobby who always slid out of trouble – marrying this pretty little lawyer. He resented that Bobby could appear pulled together when all the time he was shooting dope in his veins."

Before he left the Californian capital, the Sacramento Bee came to do an interview with him. David's one request for the August '82 story was that they don't make him "look like an asshole."

The journalist, Bob Sylva, found David sitting at his kitchen table, holding a crumpled sheet of binder paper with ideas and notes of possible questions and answers. Sylva starts by asking about his dad.

"His voice is soft, tentative, distant, a muffled plea clambering for a foothold from the bottom of an emotional pit. Words tumble out of his mouth like loose stones...Young Kennedy, his head lowered, his hands trembling noticeably, skims the page before him and attempts, haltingly to reply."

Sylva made several pertinent observations. David's digs in North Sacramento struck Sylva as having "all the charm of a college dorm." He and Paula lived amidst rented furniture, rock posters including the punk band the Plasmastics, family snapshots of the Kennedys on the fridge, and even a pet parrot they named Sputnik that they tried unsuccessfully to say, "Beam me up, Scotty!" The modest, one bedroom apartment complex had a squash court and a swimming pool on site, which David used regularly.

Physically, Sylva found David to be nervous and ill at ease during the interview. He thought him to be an "awkward, painfully shy, tentative person."

But then, in a" *moment of candor, his vulnerability palpable, Kennedy speaks about himself, his problems of the past, his hopes for the future, and hints at the pressure. Left unsaid, but explicit still, is his vital need to be understood. Then his unmistakable Kennedy face, with its sturdy jaw, gentle mouth, sunny splash of freckles, and soft blue eyes that often dance circles to circumvent contact, pulls back and turns sour.*
"*...The subject shifts. Another tack is taken. Kennedy is again importuned to open up about himself...He resists. He's gently pressed. And then not so gently. He reluctantly complies, and his gaze returns to the page. His eyes scan both sides, as he searches for answers.*"

Asked what he would like to do with his life, David replies that *writing, especially journalism had long attracted him. He thought he'd like to specialize in issues of public policy. He said he felt the family pressure to amount to something.* Silva asked David what his mother would like him be. "President," David answered shrugging his shoulders, as a smile broadened across his face. "The Kennedy name opens up a lot of doors," David said. 'Sometimes doors that I don't want opened."

David told the journalist that he had made the first steps toward fulfilling his professional ambitions. He would move, he said, back to Boston and Harvard very shortly.

Sylva writes:

"*For the most part, Kennedy quietly sits there – nervous, apprehensive, with a perplexed look on his face and patiently explains over and over again, 'I'm pretty much of a regular guy. My life is like anyone else's – except that I have a famous last name.' He then takes a deep drag off a cigarette, and anxiously awaits a response.*

Behind Blue Eyes

> *"When asked if the responsibility of representing his father's image, of being privy to the legacy, ever proves overwhelming at times, David Kennedy lowers his eyes, pauses for a moment, and in a soft affecting voice, plainly whispers 'yes.'"*

"I went to cut David's hair the night before he left and to say goodbye to him," Nancie Alexander recalled. "I told him I'd take them to the airport. I borrowed my girlfriends beat up Volkswagen van, but when I got to David's place, I had to wake them up. When we finally got to the airport, I saw something strange happen. Here's David running to the ticket counter with his beautiful black leather jacket on, and his shirttails flying, and his hair all messed up, and the ticket agents are being very rude to him. You could see them thinking, 'Look at this punk kid.' All of a sudden he gave his name and it came up on the computer screen. *Kennedy, David.* And they suddenly realized who they were dealing with. I was standing right next to David and I saw this look come across his face. It was a look of disappointment. All of a sudden they realized he was a Kennedy and they were very nice and very polite and falling over themselves to help him with his luggage. And that upset him because David thought he was nothing, that he didn't deserve any fanfare. He hated being sick, and believed that he wasn't good enough to be a Kennedy. I kissed him goodbye and then I watched him board the plane and then I cried."

Nancie Alexander wouldn't see David again.

The restorative atmosphere in California had stirred his ambition. Completing his B.A. degree at Harvard was never far from his thoughts since leaving it unfinished in the 70s. It was time to turn those plans into reality. "Some people don't think I can do it," David said of his return to Harvard. "I want to prove that I can." While he saw his renewed hope for the future as a new beginning, it was really the beginning of the end. He would have 18 months to live.

Behind Blue Eyes

PART 5: FALTERING STEPS
1982 - 1984

17. Back to Boston

September 1982 brought David back to the east coast and with it a new opportunity for progress. He and girlfriend Paula Scully set up an Apartment together in Boston's Beacon Hill. His immediate aim was to successfully complete his degree; he felt it had been hanging over his head for too long - it was time to get it finished. His studies came to symbolize his efforts to turn his life around - perhaps the tide would turn as a result. David hoped that by gaining his B.A. the turbulent rollercoaster that had so often threatened to derail, would somehow follow a more orderly path. Maybe this would bring him the professional progress he so desired and a much needed stability that his family relationships had so often lacked. At twenty-seven, the big three-o seemed to him to be looming very large in his sights. David sensed that time was running out for him to prove that he was worthy of bearing the Kennedy name. Some of his younger siblings and cousins were leap-frogging him into professions and marriages, increasing his sense of anxiety.

Two themes seemed to running in tandem at this juncture of his life. One was the need to make something of his life in accordance with his family's expectations. The crushing weight of the Kennedy legacy and how best to work within it was still a dominant theme in his life. How to carve out a niche for himself without the much sought after guidance and love of his father, who understood his shyness and sensitivity, was a continual source of pain. People were always saying that he was the brightest of the RFK children – the golden haired boy, the gifted one. It seemed at times to overwhelm him, as he felt the likelihood of his successful navigation of the problem was getting harder to bring to fruition with each passing year.

"We all are supposed to make something of ourselves because we have been given so much," he said at the time. "I don't know how I'm going to do that yet. The first thing I have to do is find some way to help others...somehow."

The second major theme in David's life was his frustration as to how his life had turned out thus far. He was embarrassed that his behavior had at times hurt those closest to him.

"I bet (one of his brothers) thinks I don't care about him, but I love him," David said. "I know I've given him – given all of them really – a hard time."

"I'm ashamed at being laughed at as a junkie," he added. "And I'm determined to set my life straight because I've come too close to checking out and I don't want to go that way."

His mantra became something along the lines of "I don't want to embarrass my family anymore." If he couldn't succeed he reasoned, than not doing anything that would cause himself undue embarrassment would become a goal. Always extremely hard on himself, drink and drugs had become a way of escaping from the disgrace he felt he had brought the family. A friend says of David's despair, "He really did believe that everyone in the family regarded him merely as a skeleton to be kept closeted."

While still in Sacramento during the summer of 1982, David approached Harvard about recommencing his studies. They were supportive, but skeptical, he later told a former classmate. The friend wondered whether going back to Harvard was such a good idea. Wouldn't it provoke unpleasant memories? And what of the family members that had preceded him? The pressure of living up to the ghosts of the past would surely prove difficult. But David was emphatic. No, Harvard was where he needed to be. There was unfinished business there. What better way to prove himself worthy than to succeed in one of the world's most prestigious academic environments?

In order to prove he could function well and was clear-headed, Harvard advised David to hold down a job for a 6-month period. The Kennedy family stepped in and arranged an internship for him at the Boston based Atlantic Monthly. In December 1982, he was hired by Mortimer Zuckerman to work with senior editor Michael Curtis. David's job initially, was to read unsolicited manuscripts, but found the work boring and didn't have an aptitude for it.

"Over time, it became clear that was not going to be his strong suit." Curtis recalled. "He simply had no experience as a critic of literary form…He was also having some trouble just sitting down and working for a sustained period of time. He needed to be up around and walking...I don't know if this was drug related for not. He'd go out and walk around the block...and clear his head."

A co-worker, Maureen Foley, had her own impressions of David during his time at the Monthly. "He was very sensitive, articulate and witty," she said. "I don't think he compared himself with his brothers and sisters and cousins. I think he knew he was a different kind of person. And he had an urgent desire to prove himself."

David flew to California for a short break over the weekend of March 4-6, 1983, after being approached by author David Horowitz, who was writing a book on the Kennedy family. Horowitz, who lived in nearby Berkeley, met with David for an initial "meet and greet" at a British themed restaurant called Victoria Station in Marin on Sunday, March 6. "David had started drinking again," writes Laurence Leamer. "His face was red and he was trembling. When Horowitz looked into David's eyes, he thought they looked full of anger and fear. 'I want to tell your story David, from your point of view," said Horowitz..."You've been scapegoated in this family, and I mean, you're the one who takes the blame for everything, and that's really unfair.'"

Horowitz was keen to interview David but thought his condition would not allow for a productive meeting, as David was "sadly slurring a potpourri of words..." Horowitz persisted though. When David got back to Boston, Paula Scully says Horowitz called several times before David relented to an actual interview. They sat down on Monday, April 4, 1983. "I met Horowitz [with David] and we gave him dinner at David's apartment in Boston," she said. "I left as soon as I saw his tape recorder. I didn't even want a cough of mine on the tape..."

"Horowitz was about the only person in David's world ready to listen to him with a sympathetic ear," Leamer thought. "And once he began to talk he could hardly stop." Over the following 4 months, Horowitz conducted numerous interviews with David. For his part, David would come to be haunted by his co-operation - but that was still 12 months down the road.

Back at the Atlantic Monthly, Curtis reassigned David to work in the filing and mail room, doing clerical, mail deliveries and other odd errands. "He was a willing worker, not necessarily a skilled worker," Curtis concluded. "But he was doing rather unglamorous work. He struck all of us as someone who wanted very much to go back to school...and his wish to put all of this behind him. He needed to show he could do reasonably well...During his few months here, he made a number of friends. Everybody who worked with him was touched by him. He was gaunt and showed the results of a nasty life...He was struggling against a lot of demons and only with moderate success. We felt poignant about it. Those of us who saw him found it impossible not to like him and sympathize with his on-going struggle and hoped he'd make a go of it."

Though David was off drugs at this point, he was still drinking heavily. Since landing in Sacramento three years previously, his alcohol consumption had steadily risen and become more dysfunctional.

"He would frequently come to work looking as if he'd been up all night, his shirt untucked, often without a tie," a colleague said. "His eyes were often bloodshot. He sometimes had the smell of alcohol on him and at times he would have difficulty focusing or talking. Sometime he would fall asleep at his desk and be sent home. Sometime he did not show up for work."

"He was clearly struggling with his drinking," Michael Curtis explained. "He sometimes would appear at work in a daze, not speaking clearly, his shirt outside his pants. From time to time he would fall asleep at his desk."

Again, defying his detractors, he managed to complete his 6 month internship at the end of May 1983, increasing his family's sense of optimism over his future. He immediately enrolled in summer school at Harvard commencing the next month.

There was a sense that David's life was on the upswing after a stabilizing, but quiet past couple of years. One woman, describing herself as a life-long friend says that he continued to enjoy an active life, regardless of his circumstances.

"He was adventurous, fond of skiing and sailing," she said. "It may sound cliché, but he did love to play touch football. He was also fond of scuba-diving, jet-skiing and nice things like whipping around in his BMW.

"He had a nice apartment on Beacon Street," the friend said. "He was a very funny person, very bright, but he'd had setbacks."

His relationship with his family, his mother particularly, had noticeably improved. "It took me a long time to understand her," David said of his mother, "but that doesn't mean I love her any less."

He hung out at his old haunts during the summer of '83. Paul Talbott, part owner of the Parting Glass Irish Pub in Hyannis, remembered David's well behaved demeanor.

"The only thing I can tell you about David Kennedy is when he was in this establishment, he always conducted himself like a gentleman," Talbott said. "I could say, 'David, you have had enough to drink' and he would just say, 'OK, Mr. Talbott,' and leave. He came in here a lot. He did drink too much. He did a lot of things too much, but he was always a gentleman...He wasn't a punk and I think he respected people. He really did...But I think they expected more from him, like my father or your father would expect more from me or you."

A friend says, "He was so damned troubled. No one could reach him. He was just brilliant. As far as I'm concerned, he was the most brilliant of Bobby's kids. But he was so lonely. So out of touch with everybody. Even when he was off drugs, he'd lost touch with reality."

Paul McGowan, a local Cape Cod resident, met David during this period of his life. "He just wanted to play down the Kennedy part of and be one of the boys," he said.

"He talked a lot," McGowan continued. "He said he had done some writing. Politics was never a big part of his life that I knew of, but then I just had a couple of beers with him now and again."

McGowan said David "didn't or act like he was from money. Dave never drove a Corvette and he didn't wear diamond rings. He wore Izod shorts that looked like it had been worn six times before."

"One night we were out here and he didn't have a place to stay," McGowan recalled. "He didn't have a credit card and he had a three-party check that he couldn't get cashed, but he wasn't about to knock on grandma's door. You think they have so much, but you really have to wonder."

Chip Mitchell, a bartender at the Parting Glass during David's time in Massachusetts, thought David felt the strain of living up to the family's expectations. "I guess he was under a lot of pressure. All the aggravation in his life, all the tragedy. He just didn't have anyone to turn to."

In mid-summer, during one of their last interviews, David Horowitz told his subject something his research had uncovered." I'm going to tell you something I know," he said. Lem Billings had been using drugs with the younger members of the family and RFK jr had developed a heroin problem. Horowitz told David that he knew the Kennedy family would blame him for the revelations.

David called Bobby jr and told him of Horowitz's intentions. David called Horowitz back and told him Bobby wouldn't be talking to him again if he revealed the drug usage of the third generation. Bobby effectively told the world himself when he was busted for heroin possession two months later.

"David flipped out completely when he heard that information he supplied to the authors, which candidly describes drug use in the family, was going to be used," said an insider. "He didn't think the material would be used, and he felt ashamed and guilty for exposing family secrets. He was angry at himself for talking so freely. His mother Ethel was furious at him, and Ted hit the ceiling. David felt pain and hopelessness..." The family had apparently tried to get David to see a Boston attorney in order for him to retract his comments - he refused.

David also spent time in Los Angeles during the summer of 83. His friend David Narva, who owned a boutique in Palm Springs, said they spent time visiting the grave of sex goddess Marilyn Monroe - with whom he says, David felt a strong affinity.

"We went to her grave at David's insistence," Narva recalls. "He was surprised when I told him that I'd never visited her crypt and insisted on taking me there."

"I can't believe you've never visited her grave," David told his friend. "Whenever I'm in LA, I always stop there. She and my father were very close and I feel a special link to her.

"My Dad talked about Marilyn a lot," David furthered. "I was just a little kid when she died, but I feel like I know her from my dad's stories.

"Her death was such a blow to him," David remembered. "Her life was so tragic. On the surface, it looked to the world as if she had everything - fame, money, beauty," David said. "But no one understood the secret agonies she was suffering. It's not easy being in the spotlight. People expect so much more from you. I identify with Marilyn," David stated. "That's why I feel drawn to her grave site. It's strange, but I think I understand her death. The world was not made for someone as sensitive as her."

"When David left the cemetery, he was crying," says Narva.

His last summer wasn't just about friends. David made the conscious decision to improve the relationship with his family, which had been strained in recent years. He was said to be delighted that the affection was reciprocated and that their previous estrangement wasn't permanent.

"It was family, family, family for David after that," Paula Scully stated. The family member he spent the most time with was his younger sister Courtney and her husband Jeff Ruhe, who were based in California.

At the same time his studies recommenced, David began seeing a psychiatrist. "At the beginning my shrink would ask me about my father," David recalled. "And I'd go on about the pictures on the wall. Finally we talked it out and I began to admit where all the hurt in me was coming from."

He also admitted some aspects of the Kennedy legacy still did not appeal to him. "My uncle Jack and my father always used to quote that Englishman – politics is the noblest profession," David said. "To me, politics is crap. That's the main thing, maybe the only thing I've learned in my life. America needs a rest from the Kennedys and vice versa."

David was always careful at not living with delusions of grandeur – he was acutely aware of his life situation. "I think we've spent a lot of time and money and energy in this family doing things for the country and look where it got us," he asserted. "But I know what this family means to many people and I think that's important. The price on us though was very high...They expect too much."

His brother Bobby would dismiss such comments, whenever he spoke of the legacy in this way, as "junkie talk." David would immediately reply, "You're a junkie too. You just haven't admitted it yet." But Bobby too would succumb to the pressure of family expectation.

On Sunday, September 11th, 1983, Bobby Jr was on a Republic Airlines flight from Minneapolis to Rapid City to seek treatment for his heroin addiction. During the flight, Bobby became seriously ill. It's believed he had an overdose in the plane's washroom. The pilots radioed ahead for medical attention, but he was feeling better by the time they landed. He was taken to the airport's VIP room and left after three hours. Police obtained a search warrant for luggage they had kept and found a small quantity of heroin. He was duly charged on September 16th and pleaded guilty. He received two years probation and community service.

David wasn't happy that his brother had suffered a major downfall, it was the fact he anticipated that his own struggle would engender greater sympathy. His first reaction was "I'm not alone anymore." However Bobby enjoyed his family's full support as he put himself into rehab in New Jersey. It was a life milestone for Bobby as he turned his life around. He would channel his energy into environmental issues, an area where he had long maintained an interest. David understood that the family's sympathy was with his brother during his first drug related crisis. However, it was painful to see the love and support this fostered in his family. Bobby was said to have told close friends that he regretted not getting his life together sooner so he could have helped David. He told a journalist in

2006 that the time in question "was hideous" and his brother was his best friend.

Also, Bobby continued to make professional progress during his addiction. He passed the bar exam, albeit on his 2nd attempt and was an assistant district attorney in New York. He seemed to walk more assuredly than David.

But perhaps more importantly, he was able to keep his growing addiction, said to be equal, if not worse than David's, under wraps from the media's increasingly tabloid clutches. In a family that cared so much about its public image, it was a salient factor in the family's lack of critical judgment. It appeared, from the family's perspective, that Bobby was making a more successful attempt at living with the pressure of expectation, despite his demons. A setback for David seemed almost certain.

When contacted about his brother's drug bust, David was philosophical. "He was the best and the brightest," he said. "There's no doubt about that. If things had been different, he might have made it. As it was, there was no way. Even so, Bobby was our last illusion."

"David was too fragile," his former girlfriend Claire told this author. "He had too much heart and even guilt. I talked to him soon after Bobby's arrest and in a warped way he was pretty glad that Bobby had finally lost his cool. He didn't want harm to come to Bobby, David just resented that no one really saw how messed up Bobby was and dumped all the guilt on David."

The brotherly competitiveness that characterized much of their youth was still evident as they prepared to exit their twenties.

"You cannot overemphasize just how much David felt he needed to beat Bobby," Claire asserts. "David could beat the heck out of Bobby in sports. He said that irked Bobby, since being an athlete was synonymous with being a Kennedy.

"Funny, I was just watching some celebrity ski event," Claire continued. "Bobby and Kerry were both skiing in it. Bobby was a dead heat against a pro. He's talented, but to know how David would kick a rooster tail of snow in Bobby's face as he came up a few seconds short was a big deal to David."

A day after Bobby was formally charged, on September 17, 1983, Kennedy cousin, Sydney Lawford, sister of Chris, was the next of the third generation to tie the knot. It was a typical lavish affair held at the Kennedy compound at Hyannis Port. David had seemingly reached a more stable point in his life, despite ongoing anxieties. He was getting along better with his family, Harvard beckoned and he was drug free, for now - although he was still drinking. The physical toll of his abuse was becoming startlingly evident. But he was still defying the odds.

"David showed up looking a lot like the beat up Pontiac he had driven down from New Hampshire," Chris Lawford writes in his autobiography, Symptoms of Withdrawal. "The fact he had no license didn't bother him in the slightest. When I asked him how he managed it, he looked at me with the quizzical contempt he had elevated to an art form and said, 'Man, you don't need a license to drive.' It was pure David. I sat with my best friend and my father that night, knowing we were far from what we could be. David's bravado was still evident, but he had changed. I could see in his eyes that he was beaten, and although there was a thirty-plus age difference between my dad and him, they both looked like club fighters at the end of a punishing fifteen rounds – powerless to dodge the inevitable outcome. David regaled us with the story of how he got me fired at Universal Studios and we continued our ancient argument as to who was smarter while we waited for the (sun to come up). I had the feeling I was seeing him for the last time."

Another person who observed David could also see his poor physical condition. "When David went to his cousin Sydney Lawford's wedding, he looked pitiful, totally wasted away," the friend remembered. "He walked over to where Jackie Onassis was standing and the look in his eyes of, 'Please be my friend. I'm trying to do better.' He hugged a person who was standing next to Jackie and started crying. He told the person, 'I don't have many friends, but it's great to have a friend like you.' Jackie felt sorry for him. It was embarrassing to watch."

He started classes that autumn at Harvard, making terrific academic progress. Though his major was in history, he also took units in Archeology and Anthropology. He called his classes, in his self-deprecating way, "mummies for dummies" and "monkeys for junkies."

John Marquand was assistant dean and David's academic advisor, and became a close friend over the next several months. Marquand said David showed tremendous potential, saying "he was doing very well in every regard." However, Marquand says that though exceptionally bright, David had some difficulty channeling his enormous talent into a productive area. They discussed several possible career paths – journalism, law, teaching, business and even politics. Marquand says that David was "an optimistic and cheerful person, serious-minded, yet witty." The academic didn't think RFK's death played overly on David's mind, saying that "he did not brood."

In October of '83 his old friend from Sacramento, Dave Kelley, spent some time with him in Boston. Crashing at David's Beacon Hill apartment, Kelley said that they watched the World Series baseball. Kelley says the two of them went out to dinner and thought David to be in good spirits. "He sounded really good," Kelley said. "I thought he was getting his act together. He sounded excited about finishing school."

Another old friend who saw him at this time thought he looked terrific, mentally and physically. "He was in great shape, looking tanned and gorgeous," she thought.

What happened that triggered the backslide into drugs and depression is not clear. But two months later at Christmas, when the family gathered once again at Aspen, Colorado for their annual end-of-year holiday, it was clear that things were not going well for David. He was seen drinking heavily at several local establishments, and seemed particularly downcast when an ex-girlfriend bumped into him.

"He was having some moments like that last Christmas where he seemed totally defeated," she observed to this author. "We ran into each other at a bar on the slopes and a few times in town at dinner. We had a ten minute conversation when he cornered me as I left a restaurant one night...He was sweet, and engaging and wanted to make sure I was okay...David was drinking pretty hard when I left the bar," the woman recalled.

"He was at the bar itself, and was pretty morose and defeated. He had one of his beat down moods going on. He was not looking great; he was way too skinny and tired and haggardly looking."

18. 1984

"I keep praying that each year will be a better one for us," Sargent Shriver said in his customary New Year's toast at the Shriver home, with many family present, David included. "I hope this will be that year," Sarge said.

As 1984 dawned, it saw David's withdrawal from the spring semester at Harvard. It would be the last time he set foot on campus. He told friends he needed time out in order to get his life together.

"He was back on heroin," a friend commented sadly. "...He'd succumbed to the killer drug once more."

However, there was much admiration from some quarters for the quiet strength he continued to show. His brother Michael said at the time that David "has shown more courage than any of the rest of us. Something in him wants to live and come back. It's just that he has had such a hard, hard time."

One day in January 1984, Paula Scully uncovered the famous photo of David taken by his Aunt Jackie standing in front of the White House in the June 14, 1968 edition of LIFE magazine. President Kennedy had signed the bottom of the picture with the inscription "A future president inspects his property." When Paula showed David the photo, she recalled that "it put a big smile on his face. He started reminiscing about playing with his Uncle Jack that day and beating up Bobby Shriver." David asked Paula to phone LIFE for a copy, but when the Picture Service manager called to arrange delivery, David failed to get in touch. 3 months later, at David's wake, his Aunt Jackie mentioned the day she took the photo, and Paula responded simply with, "I already know."

One morning in February, Ethel walked into the drawing room of Hickory Hill to find a picture of her and Bobby from their wedding day placed on the coffee table instead of hanging in its place on the wall. Upon examination, she discovered a powdery residue on it. Clearly, someone had been using the glass to snort cocaine. In her mind, this was one of the most sacrilegious things she'd ever heard of...She was "absolutely inconsolable for hours."

That night, David didn't show up for the dinner, usually not a big deal. But this night, the Shrivers were holding a meeting with the third generation, hoping to get them involved in some philanthropic activities during the coming year. It was to Ethel's considerable embarrassment that her 4th born was absent. Afterward, he finally made an appearance, looking tired and disheveled. Throughout the time Sarge spoke about the importance of public service, mother and son glared at one another.

Finally after Sargent finished his talk... Ethel pulled David into the kitchen by his arm. Concerned about a potential blow up between the two, a couple of his siblings followed them, as did two of his friends. "How dare you show up looking like this?" Ethel demanded to know of David. "*What is wrong with you?*"

David didn't answer. He just stood in front of his mother looking defeated.

"And was it *you* who used the wedding picture of me and your father to do drugs?" she demanded. "It *was* you wasn't it? Who else?" she asked. "*Who else?*"

Still no answer.

"Answer me," Ethel demanded, looking at her son with angry eyes. But now she was crying. "You answer me this very instant, David Kennedy!" David took a deep breath and let it out slowly. Then, seemingly very ashamed of himself and with tears in his eyes, he very quietly said, "I love you mom. That's all I've got."

Ethel seemed stunned. The two just stared at each other for a few moments. "Oh my God, David," Ethel said, sounding almost winded by the surprise comment. Then, with tears streaming down her face, she took her son into her arms and hugged him as tightly as she could.

"A few months before he died he called me for the last time," a former girlfriend told this author. "He wanted to save me from my husband. He could tell he was mean to me, and where I was pregnant. He wanted me to bring my daughter and come stay with him. He said he'd raise the baby as his own. That was the kind of guy he was. He was pretty messed up though. I told him I couldn't do that and he got upset with me about it. Thought it meant I didn't care about him, and that I didn't trust him. I guess his paranoia was oozing a little. Still, he said we could help each other. It was the last time we talked."

With the publication date of the Collier / Horowitz book fast approaching, the family became concerned about skeletons being dragged out of proverbial closets. David's contribution to the tome became front and center in his life again and something of an albatross around his neck. The brewing storm clouds looked set to open.

12 months previously, when first approached by the authors, he had initially been happy to unlock the family secrets, telling the authors, "I've always been the odd-man out."

"Of all the kids, he had nothing to lose," David Horowitz commented. "For David, it was like evening the score."

Hard pressure exerted by the family on David to withdraw his comments for the forthcoming book apparently had an effect. Perhaps a fear at being further ostracized from the family was the hook that reeled him into the family's line of thinking.

Some have suggested there was an ultimatum from the family, telling him to shape-up or ship out. David, however, appeared to be very motivated to a life free of drink and drugs, and went into rehab under his own steam. Gaining his health and being well was an important goal, though some think the influence of his family was a stronger factor in the process.

"He was afraid he was going to be totally abandoned by them if he didn't conquer his addictions," one insider thought. "He felt desperately unloved by his family…"

Whatever the case may be, David made a last ditch effort to try and kill the book. Several desperate phone calls were made to the authors, which were recorded on secret tapes.

A source very close to the authors who has heard the tapes, thought David sounded drugged when telling Horowitz, "I'm up to eyeballs in shit."

But it was too late. The matter was out of the authors' hands, and the publisher, Simon and Schuster, parent company of the actual publisher, Summit Books, had no intention of withdrawing what was certain to be a best-seller.

David's concern with the revelations in black and white was that he'd cut himself off from his family for good. He was desperate enough to fly out to California and try and persuade the authors in person. However, Kennedy family lawyers had argued against that idea, saying it would be better to sever all ties with the writers.

Many friends believe it was the guilt and family pressure surrounding the new book that finally took its toll on what was left of David's sobriety. He appeared to sink even deeper into a deep depression as his downward spiral continued.

It was no surprise that David's drug use crept up in conjunction with growing family disharmony and depression. After a promising past 12 months, his backslide into hard drugs was in danger on making his life a mirror image of the late 70s. David once again began spending time in New York seeking out his old haunts.

His drug dealer at this stage explained their arrangement. "I moved in with my mother, and Kennedy would call the house and ask me to buy for him," the dealer stated. "I told him to use the name 'Ritchie' when he phoned so I'd know who it was. He'd call from a downstairs phone booth, then I'd go down and meet him and buy some heroin for him..."

There was even rumors that his life was being threatened in his final months from dealers he owed money too. A close friend says the threats were real. "He was terrified," the source claimed. "The family did quietly alert the FBI and asked for an investigation - but they refused to help him pay off the dealers."

His life when in New York wasn't encouraging either. He would stay at his Grandmother Rose's apartment at 59th Street and Central Park South and shoot heroin. "Periodically he would overdose, and thrash about and make noise until someone heard and alerted the doorman to check on him," Rose's personal secretary, Barbara Gibson said. "Several times the building staff had to call the police to break in because Rose had four or five locks on the door...David apparently had used all the locks so he would not be disturbed," Gibson added.

"When I stayed in the apartment while working for Rose, evidence of David's past visits were everywhere," Gibson furthered. "All the floor lamps had their cords cut off so he could use them as tourniquets on his arm..."

Despite his nefarious lifestyle, plans were still afoot. With the previous year being taken up largely with work and study, traveling and recreation was high on the agenda of things to do this year, David told friends. He had planned a trip to the Bahamas in early May with Paula, and Hawaii was also on the cards for the summer. The lone star state of Texas was also discussed as a possible destination to visit. There was even talk of setting up a travel related business with his brothers. He told staff at the Atlantic Monthly during a quick visit to the office in February, of his plans. They thought him to be optimistic about his future, despite Harvard not working out.

"I wanted to save him," a girlfriend told this author, "but at the time I couldn't save myself – abusive marriage. I can close my eyes and hear his voice and see his eyes. I like thinking of a more innocent David, before all the hell overtook him. He was very sweet and caring and loving when he wanted to, but he always had his guard up and would be so disappointed in anyone he thought was after the Kennedy enigma. David was a buoy for me in a storm. To this day I miss him and not a day goes by I don't wish he was still here...but a healthier, happier David – not so hurt by life."

In a telephone call to Pam Kelley in early March, David wondered whether he'd ever be truly free of his addiction. He feared "life would be too boring without drinking and drugs." Pam had kicked her own drug habit in '83 and said she and David spoke at length about drugs. "I really envy you Pam," David told his ex. "You know what you want and you know how to be happy. All I am is sad."

She said she found this ironic. "He had all the things in the world available to him that money could buy," she later said, "and here he was envious of me."

"He was thinking about going skiing the next week, or doing something else exotic," Pam continued. "And I can't go any place like that, but he was the one who wanted to be like me."

Despite niggles and frustrations, he still adored his family and derived much of his happiness from spending time with them.

"He went to every family affair he ever could," Paula Scully said. "Those were the times that made him very, very happy. I'll never forget the continual grin on his face when he was around them."

Even as thirty closed in on him, one family member in particular was still very much on his mind in his last months - his dad. He told one friend, "I think about death a lot. Time hasn't erased the death of my father from my mind."

"David wanted to know everything about his father's life," Paula Scully recalled. "It was amazing how quickly he could step back almost 20 years," she said. "But then, when he'd stop talking, the void would come back. He was anguished by the loss."

"David talked about his dad constantly," said one woman who knew David in his last year. "(He spoke) of the horror of his death and how much he missed him."

David headed out to Sacramento for a 10 day trip during the first half of March. In addition to catching up with friends, he did a little spring Sierra skiing, as he told Pam Kelley he was going to do. He stayed at the house of Miles Smith, a 32yr old sales rep.

"He was happier than hell," he said of David. The two often went out to dinner or a show at Laughs Unlimited, or just simply had a night out on the town. "He was happy as a clam," Smith furthered. "He seemed like he finally had a hold on himself. We had a good time."

As soon as David got back home after his trip to California, he immediately enrolled in a rehabilitation program in the now defunct Spofford Hall, located in the small village of Spofford, New Hampshire. The facility opened its doors in 1980 and closed them ten years later. It offered (usually affluent) patients a three-to-four week intensive program in pleasant and anonymous surroundings. It was the kind of atmosphere that would appeal to David's sense of privacy.

But for all his good intentions, David's stay at Spofford Hall was brief – all of 6 days. The day after he checked in, Wednesday, March 14, he sat down to pen a poem he intended to recite at a talent show organized by the facility. He would have 6 weeks of life left to the day.

OLD SPOFFORD BLUES

PRETTY SOON WE'RE GOING TO BE FORGOTTEN
BECAUSE WE'RE ALL SO ROTTEN
THEY TRIED TO TALK US INTO SOBRIETY
BUT IN OUR MINDS WE WANT TO PARTY
NEEDLES AND LINES DANCE THROUGH OUR HEAD
AND IF WE DON'T GET OUT WE'LL ALL BE DEAD
THEY TALK ABOUT FAITH, HOPE AND GOD,
WE'VE HAD ENOUGH OF THESE CLOWNS AND GOONS
JUST GIVE ME BACK MY NEEDLES AND SPOONS
WE MEAN WELL, IT'S NO JOKE
BUT WE WOULD DO ANYTHING FOR A GRAM OF COKE
IF YOU DOUBT OUR WORD – IF YOU THINK IT'S A LIE
WE'LL TELL YOU TO FUCK OFF AND DIE
THEY SAY THAT SOME DAY WE WILL ALL BE JUST VISIONS
OF KILOS I STILL WANT TO SELL IN MY VISION
28 DAYS IS THE SPOFFORD TOUR
BUT I KNOW DEEP DOWN THE BIG H (HEROIN) IS WHAT CURES
AND NOW OUR STAY HAS BEEN TOLD
I CAN'T WAIT TO LEAVE SPOFFORD BEHIND.

"Four days after he wrote this poem," a fellow patient recalled, "David told me that his friend was up and that she smuggled in $400 worth ($830 today) of cocaine. At that point,

I went to the staff – I was serious about getting well – and told them he was in possession of cocaine. They checked his room while he was in class, found the cocaine and booted him out of the facility (the same day)."

David seemed to have derived some good from his treatment despite his shorter than anticipated stay. Pam Kelly, David's ex-girlfriend, said she spoke to him about his treatment.

"I think they had gotten through to him at Spofford," Pam said. "Because he was really listening to me and he wasn't full of bull.

"He seemed somewhat better," she thought. "He said he was hopeful. He was tired of being looked at as the Kennedy screw-up. He wanted more for himself and his family. 'I get it now that I'm totally responsible for my own problems,' he told me. 'I want to do better. I don't want to be this guy who is always so ashamed of himself and of what he is doing to his family. I will be better. I have to get better.

"You know what they told me there?" David tells Pam. "They said that I was a good person," Pam went on. "It was unbelievable that David did not see that himself and that it came as a big surprise to him. The thing that impressed him the most was that the guy who told him that didn't have any reason to – he wasn't trying to flatter a Kennedy...he was telling David the truth.

Despite seeming more optimistic about his future, there was a melancholy in his voice, Pam thought. "He was very sad," Pam recalls. "He seemed like he wanted to be clean like I was and he wanted to connect with a part of his past. I told him that he would be fine if he ever got sober and got off drugs. And the last thing I said was, 'David, in our next phone call we'll talk about happiness.'"

But he struggled on. His old journalist friend Tom Oliphant, and others, recognized the courageousness of his struggle. "He made a Herculean effort to beat drugs," the writer said admiringly. He would once again head back into rehab – his 5th stint.

"This is it, David," Ted told him. "I'm very serious. We're running out of solutions here. It's time for you to be a real

Kennedy. Kennedys don't quit; Kennedys don't fail; Kennedys don't let each other down."

Cousin Michael Skakel who had been treated at St. Mary's rehabilitation Center some years before, recommended the facility to David. On March 19th, 1984, according to Michael Skakel, he drove David to St. Mary's (taken over in 1986 by Fairview Southdale Hospital), in downtown Minneapolis. He spent a full month at the $149 per night center under the name of David Kilroy. He confirmed to his counseling group that he was indeed David Kennedy. "It was pretty obvious he was resisting," a staffer there commented. "He was in his own world. He was brought up to hide his feelings. And he was scared to death."

While inside, he formed a relationship with a young woman who was also detoxing. She claims he spoke of starting a new life with her once they were released.

"David entered the center to try and show his family he could beat his drug and booze problem," the woman recalled. "David told me, 'my family thinks I'm no good and I'll never beat my problem. They've written me off. I'm going to show them I can beat it.'

"But about a week into the program, I sensed he was giving up," she said. "Then he fell off the wagon and got heavily back into alcohol. It's easy to get in and out of the center, so he could easily pick up what he wanted. We'd talk late into the night and he told me, 'It's no good. I can't beat this problem. My family wants nothing more to do with me. All I want is to be with my father.'"

A friend remembered receiving a call from David while he was still in St. Mary's. "When David called me he was drunk," the friend stated. "His mood varied from optimistic to hopeless. He told me, 'I'm trying to get it together, but it's so difficult. I'm having a terrible time at it.' Then in uncharacteristic frankness, he blurted out,' the thing I want most in the world is the approval of my family. But they're not really trying to help me. I don't know which way to turn. What should I do?' I told him he was so drunk that he should call me back when he was sober so I could understand him. And that was the last I heard from him."

While still undergoing treatment, the first excerpts of the Peter Collier / David Horowitz book came out in Playboy magazine. He had hoped that he could unburden himself from the pressures he felt of being a Kennedy - It would work out very differently as the publication hit the stands in late March. It appeared his anxiety over the content of his interviews was well founded.

"When David read the article in Playboy, it devastated him beyond belief," Paula Scully said. "David made a mistake by talking. Everyone makes mistakes, but David didn't realize until too late how big of a mistake he had made."

Though angrily denied later on, there was a persistent rumor that the Kennedys had accused David of treason, for breaching the family trust. "One night," Nancy Narleski said, "his brothers called him a traitor and said that he wasn't worthy to bare the Kennedy name. He was crying when he told me this."

Narleski also added that "he was under tremendous pressure from his family. They were terrorizing him. They blamed him for what happened to Bobby jr. They told him he had been a bad example. David didn't even bother to point out that it was Bobby that had led him astray. He just accepted their framework and felt guilty."

While it's unlikely the relationship had become as untenable as the more tabloid reports would suggest, it appears that the relationship with his family had become tense once again. The family angrily denies that the conversation between the brothers ever took place. But in spite of this, both sides hung in there - as they always did. Their common bond being far stronger than temporary grievances.

"David could have walked away from the necessity of being a Kennedy," Horowitz said in an interview to promote his controversial book. "If he could have discovered his real self, he could have survived.

"I found David perceptive and witty," Horowitz furthered. "He never complained. He never blamed his family for his drug troubles. He internalized his pain. His family treated him as if he were a pariah…He was in a difficult emotional state...The Kennedy attitude toward David, especially from Ethel, was: 'You have brought disgrace on the family.' The Kennedy charisma came to an end at Chappaquiddick. But it was David who was continuously berated for being a disgrace."

A source close to the family however claims the authors took advantage of the family's most vulnerable member. "David thought these guys were his friends. But in fact they took his life and spread it out for the public to see. They used him," the source said.

Horowitz hit back by saying that "there was no pretense that there was any kind of friendship relationship there...David had nothing to lose and everything to gain by talking to us about his drug problem," he said.

David had soon come to regret co-operating with the authors though. "He was very disturbed with himself that he had done this," family friend Larry Newman said. "He had hurt a lot of people."

Cousin Chris Lawford thought that the publication of his interviews "was more than his fragile sobriety could tolerate...David may have been way outside the family," Lawford continued, "he may have known before any of us what a cruel joke it was to have such an illustrious legacy, but he loved his family and hurting or disappointing them was not something he could live through. There was no place for David in the family, and he could not go away to honor his authentic self. He had been in a purgatory of pain pretty much his entire life. So he did what he had always done to stop the hurt. He got high, and it killed him. He died...alone with the pain of knowing that he had disappointed the family that meant everything to him, but he could not be a part of."

He thought about his options for the future - perhaps he would start a new life with his girlfriend from St. Mary's? "Sometimes we'd talk about a future together," the woman recalled. "We planned to go to Texas after we got out. But David completed his stay at the center before me. He was supposed to go into a halfway house in Minneapolis, but he flew to Palm Beach instead (when he heard about his grandmother)."

There was also the option of getting away with Nancy Narleski. David helped Nancy plan a trip to Hawaii for the summer, using money that she would get from an insurance claim. "Just hang on until I get my money," she told David in rehab. "Then we'll get away from all of this and go to Maui."

But Narleski realized the pull of the family was too great and that he would be forever anchored to the family emotionally no matter how far he removed himself physically.

"He really couldn't conceive of being apart from them, cut off, on his own. The Kennedys were David's real addiction." Claire told this author much the same when she concluded, "he felt victimized by the family, but it was his greatest drug."

David for his part, more or less concurred when just four weeks before he passed, he wrote: "They (the Kennedys) have their own idea of reality which isn't mine, but it has a hold on me...One step forward, two steps back, two steps forward, one step back. My life keeps marshmellowing along, accepting a certain negativity."

Though he emerged from rehab refreshed, some of his old friends like John Warnecke Jr were still worried. "I was scared to death for David," Warnecke said. "There wasn't a day when I wasn't expecting someone to call me and tell me David's overdosed."

Another friend summed up David's struggle for sobriety. "He was desperate to get drugs, and desperate to get off them."

His girlfriend at St. Mary's says she was very concerned for David's welfare as he left the facility. "I'll never forget how he looked when I saw him for the last time," she said. "I could see a certain fear and hopelessness in his eyes as he left the center - a feeling that he didn't believe he was going to make it. As he walked away from me I was frightened over what was going to happen to him."

The source who heard the secret tapes says that he was still in precarious shape. "David was in worse condition than the family could ever have imagined," the source revealed. "He was now in the grip of a terrible depression. He felt that he had made a mess of his life and that nothing could help."

His childhood friend, Liza Noyes said that she had thought a lot about David since their last encounter back in 1973. "Maybe because I knew he was floundering," she said. "I would study his pictures in the newspapers and they bothered me.

"Most people lose track of their first loves," Noyes continued. "I could read about mine in People magazine. Sometimes he made the front page. It was never good news, but it was good to know he was alive somewhere."

Despite David's desire to remain out of the public eye, he was about to hit the news again. True to form, it wasn't favorable, but this time however, it would be devastating news that would shock the world.

A life of two halves – one with his father and one without.
Top: RFK funeral June 8, 1968 © AP
Bottom: 2nd year anniversary mass June 6, 1970. Pictured with brother Michael and Uncle Ted © Frank Teti

Behind Blue Eyes

Top: David nursing a broken arm June 6, 1969 © Frank Teti

Bottom: Fifteen-year-old David January 1971 © Frank Teti

High School graduation Middlesex Academy – Concord, MA, June 5, 1974 Top: with mother Ethel © UPI / Bettman Bottom: Being presented with his HS diploma from Uncle Ted © Bettman / Corbis

Behind Blue Eyes

Top: Watching a match at the RFK Pro-Celebrity Tennis Tournament in New York, August 25, 1974 © Bettman / Corbis

Bottom: David talking to his mother Ethel at the Democratic National Convention in New York – July 14, 1976 © AP

Next page: David at the 60th birthday commemorations for JFK – Brookline, MA – May 29, 1977 © AP

Behind Blue Eyes

Top: David with addiction specialist Dr. Margaret Patterson and husband George (aka Patla), in Sussex, England, late autumn 1978
Bottom: David with Rachel Ward and friends – April 29, 1979 © UPI

24-year-old David at New York City nightclub Xenon, June 1979 © AP

Behind Blue Eyes

Top: David with drug counselor Donald Juhl in Sacramento, CA – March 15, 1980 © UPI / Bettman
Bottom: the author's favorite photo - taken in 1980 © Stan Shaffer

Top: At the RFK Pro-Celebrity Tennis Tournament at Hyannis Port, MA – 8/21/81 © Brian Quigley; Bottom: Being interview by the Sacramento Bee – August 27, 1982 © Mitch Toll / Sacramento Bee

Behind Blue Eyes

Top: Arriving at Cousin Sydney Lawford's wedding at Our Lady of Victory Church, Centreville, MA – 9/13/83 © Russell Turiak / Getty Images. Bottom: 28-year-old David in his final months © Christopher Kennedy Lawford

Behind Blue Eyes

PART 6: FINAL DAYS
April 19-25, 1984

"I think about death a lot. Time hasn't erased the death of my father from my mind...My family thinks I'm no good and that I'll never beat my problem. They've written me off...I'm trying to get it together, but it's so difficult. I'm having a terrible time at it...The thing I want most in the world is the approval of my family...But they want nothing more to do with me. All I want is to be with my father."

David Kennedy April 1984

The signs were unmistakable. Fifteen years of drug and alcohol abuse had taken an alarming toll on the twenty-eight year-old son of Bobby Kennedy. Looking years older, David Anthony Kennedy was a young man living in an old body. Charles Hamilton, a Palm Beach drug counselor, says, "David was abusing his life to the point where there was no return." It appeared as though he was about to be engulfed by the undertow.

He never gave up on himself however - in spite of the odds or other people's perceptions. He always seemed to find a way to pick himself up from the canvas. Realizing the road block of drugs was impeding his progress, he sought help again in navigating a path through the obstacles. This time he checked into St. Mary's Hospital and Rehabilitation Center (now Fairview Southdale Hospital) in downtown Minneapolis on March 19th, 1984 to once again try and combat his addictions.

Despite it all, he was still looking ahead. He was determined to show his family he could well and be well saying to one friend in rehab, "they've written me off. But I'm going to show them I can beat it."

Paula Scully also confirmed that David was still feeling optimistic about his future despite the hiccups along the way.

"He had plans for his life," she said. He was going to write John Seigenthaler to see if he could spend the summer working at the Nashville Tennessean, and he was thinking of going to Boston University to study journalism, which was something that really interested him..."

Apart from getting his writing up and happening, two other issues were front and center for David in his final days. Both had their roots and consequences in the family. The first was RFK Jr.

While in rehab, David thought of the support his brother had received after his recent drug bust and subsequent rehabilitation and it bothered him. He wanted Bobby well, but he also wanted sympathy for his own struggle which he felt was largely being ignored. He spoke with David Horowitz, who was co-authoring a book for which David had fully cooperated.

"David had called from [rehab]...to ask me for my advice," Horowitz stated. "He was distressed at the attention the family had paid to Bobby's plight, which contrasted with the way they had ostracized him when his own addiction made headlines... "The pain in David's voice when he related this was evident," Horowitz furthered. "I reminded him that he was marked as the family scapegoat, the one they would always point to as the Kennedy who had 'dragged the family name in the mud.' I urged him to make a separate peace with them and remove himself from the circle of their scorn. He could go back to California and make a new life for himself. But David could not break free."

A second major theme occupying David's mind in his final days involved David Horowitz directly. The author was involved with David through most of the previous spring and summer conducting interviews for a forthcoming book. He was very anxious as to how he would be portrayed - he remembered little of the "stream of consciousness" style of his interviews. He thought initially his comments would be largely off the record, but was told by Horowitz they would not be. He felt ill-prepared for the publicity awaiting him.

When the first excerpts of those interviews first emerged in the public domain, David had been in St. Mary's only about a week and doing well.

"But the [excerpt] in Playboy was the down point in his life," Paula Scully thought. "It was like taking ten steps back."

Scully says she watched him as he read the excerpt. "My God," he said shaking his head. "This is awful, it's trash." Scully thought the article and subsequent book demonstrated another example, "of David being exploited.

"He felt betrayed and used," Paula said. "But there was nothing he could do about it because it had already been published."

However, many believe it wasn't so much the content that upset him; it was the family's reaction that proved to be so devastating. Their negative stand on David's participation in the forthcoming book would have a profound effect on the events that followed.

As he was preparing for the next stage in his rehabilitation – a move into a halfway house, David's grandmother took a turn for the worse.

"We all knew that Mrs. Kennedy was very ill," Gerald Beebe, spokesman for the Brazilian Court Hotel stated. "Everyone in town knows that. So we understood that this was going to be a special holiday."

The timing was very unfortunate for David, because he was clearly in need of further treatment. Palm Beach was hardly the place for a man delicately balancing on the hire wire of sobriety. Though they weren't to know it at the time of course, Rose went on to live for another decade.

"David had flown into Palm Beach when news first circulated in the family about Rose's failing health," one insider stated.

The matriarch's increasing frailty gave the family cause for the gravest concern at the time. The younger members of the Kennedys were especially encouraged to make the trip down to Florida in what was expected to be Rose's last Easter.

THURSDAY, APRIL 19

After a month long stay, David checked out of the $149 per day ($350 today) treatment facility today,. Ex-girlfriend, fashion photographer, Paula Scully says: "I saw him when he left and he was in very good spirits. The treatment had done him a lot of good. It had been the best place in the world for

David. He was completely clean of drugs when he went to Florida..."

Not all the Kennedys had ventured down to Palm Beach but many did, including the families of Pat Lawford, Eunice Shriver and Jean Smith. David's brother Joe II, among other younger members of the family, was present also. There were reports some of the members from the 3rd generation stayed at a hotel elsewhere.

Contrary to the belief that David was such an outcast and cause for "rancor and unpleasantness" that he wasn't allowed to stay with the family, there simply wasn't the space. There is strong evidence that David was keen to stay elsewhere.

"Family members believe that David decided not to stay at the house because he would not be able to have drugs, booze or a lot of friends there," one insider suggested.

Regardless, David found himself staying at the up market Brazilian Court Hotel, some five miles (8km) away. Cleveland politician and Kennedy family friend, Timothy Hagan arranged for a complimentary suite of rooms with hotel owner, Dennis Heffernan, a former Cleveland resident. Heffernan had also been active in democratic circles, working on Teddy's 1980 presidential bid.

Heffernan received a phone call requesting the rooms the day before David was due to check in. "My friend Tim Hagan, told me that some members of the Kennedy family would be staying at my hotel for an Easter holiday and he asked me to take care of them," Heffernan recalled.

The suite would have normally cost $250 per night (more than $500 today) and had two inter-connected rooms, one of the better available suites it was said - with twin beds in both. To get to his room, David would have strolled through the Australia Avenue entrance Southern courtyard of palm trees, flowers and white tables under yellow umbrellas, which came of color under the spring sunset.

It was a beautiful spring night with the temperature having dropped to a comfortable level – warm, but bearable. As the taxi dropped RFK's fourth born at the door of the Brazilian Court Hotel, Josephine Dampier, the hotel manager's secretary, saw David as he checked in late on the Thursday night.

"David was like a Zombie when he arrived," she thought. "He was really out of it."

Another staffer had a similarly unenthusiastic first impression. "David's face was pale and drawn," he said. "His cut-off jeans, sweatshirt and dirty sneakers looked as though they should've been worn by a bum.

"He was a mess," the male staffer furthered. "He was wasted and physically drained. He was about 6 feet 2 (188cm) but skinny. But it was his face that was really scary. It was a kid's face – but (prematurely) old. It was grey and saggy, like someone had drained all the blood out of it."

David is not seen by the staff for the remainder of the evening. It is suspected he retires to his room. It was a low key start to his Easter vacation. But it didn't take him long to get into the swing of things.

Opinions vary among the staff as to David's conduct over the next week. A few thought he was out to deliberately self-destruct.

"I watched him deteriorate over those six amazingly tragic days," one staffer concluded. "It was like watching a demolition squad take down a building!"

Other employees, however, paint a favorable picture of David during his stay. One said that he did indeed appear to pace his drinking steadily.

"While he drank some, he was never wildly drunk." The female worker, who is employed poolside, dismissed the talk of David's constant inebriation as due to fellow employees like Violet Rose, a Scottish woman, who "talks and makes a lot of judgments." She mentioned that David usually had "a couple of drinks in the afternoon, but he didn't always drink liquor. Sometimes he had a (soda)."

"He was a polite young man," another hotel maid stated. "I never saw any whiskey bottles in his room, but he did seem to drink a lot of sodas."

However, he didn't just confine his drinking to the Brazilian Court. Bar staff at other local watering holes said David would pop in and have a couple of drinks – usually double vodkas on the rocks, then head to another bar before returning a few hours later.

Most of the media reports decided to run with the unfavorable view of David. Their often dramatic content telling of the subject being in a constant "alcoholic haze" during his time in the resort town - on something of a "mindless, self-destructive orgy." And that he started his day by downing shots at the bar by 8 a.m. and within the hour resembled a "transient off the street."

Of course, most of this is sensationalist fiction from the tabloids. Only brief glimpses of fact are shown amidst the misinformation. This final section of the book aims to be the definitive account of David's final movements, emotions and behavior as the timeline to his death is reconstructed in never before seen depth.

One salient fact that Heffernan tells us, is that in addition to the bar not opening until 11am, David was rarely seen emerging earlier than late morning. And no firsthand account can place him beginning to imbibe until the early afternoon. While there can be no doubt that David did drink heavily at times, his partying was far from the 16-hour daily marathons that some have been erroneously depicted. However it did steadily deteriorate as the week progressed.

David was particularly careful to disguise some of his activities when in the presence of his family, especially his youngest brother. When at the Brazilian Court, where to David at least, all eyes seemed to be focused upon him, he was considerably more measured (or perhaps more sly) in his behavior. A barman says that if Doug was around David would consume only soda or water, but if he wasn't, it was straight back into the vodka, urgently gulping down a shot. He would even try and give those watching him a bum-steer by switching drinks. "I'd say, 'Do you want a cocktail?' And if his brother was around, he'd say, 'No, no no.' Five minutes later he'd come and get me and say he wanted a double."

The hotel management was quick to defend David's conduct. They recall him being in control while in their presence, although admitting his frequency of the bar. Dennis

Heffernan regularly bumped into David in the final days of his life and had a chance to observe his behavior first hand.

"He swam more than once every day," Heffernan said. "I would see him three or four times a day. He had a few drinks during the day, but I didn't say, 'my God, this guy's an alcoholic.' I never saw him where his speech was slurred, or when I would have to say, 'He's had too much...And there is nothing to substantiate a report that he was wallowing in booze," However, Heffernan admitted David was a daily visitor to the bar and had several drinks while there.

"There is every indication that he was consuming his share of vodka," Heffernan conceded, but quickly qualified, "but not an extraordinary amount."

Heffernan also made it clear that he didn't see David, "take a misstep (or) stagger or anything...I never saw him doing push-ups or back flips, but he seemed ok—not in the peak of health, but ok."

General Manager Geoffrey Temple, "felt him to be a fine young man "who was "quite pleasant and very well mannered and very polite" during his time at the hotel.

Hotel spokesman, Gerald Beebe found David's behavior to be "calm, and quiet and his dress to be certainly within the bounds of a young man on holiday. He appeared in good health and, to the best of our knowledge, should no signs of unusual or excessive behavior...He never appeared drunk or disorderly."

"I grew up with kids who are heroin addicts," Heffernan added. "He didn't look like that. Not once did I see him really sloppy."

Though at times he overdid the partying, mostly though, it remained a steady constant during his final week. The chill and sobriety of Minnesota must have seemed a lifetime away.

FRIDAY, APRIL 20

The next day saw the arrival of Doug Kennedy, David's youngest brother and his Georgetown prep school friend Derrick Evans. Both 17 year-olds stayed in David's suite - one of ten multi-rooms in the plush establishment; and all three often shared meals together.

"I saw them in the dining room occasionally and in the lounge," said Josephine Dampier. "To my knowledge, it was the first time any of the Kennedys had stayed here."

Dennis Heffernan said David approached him on Friday morning and asked him about buying a tape recorder. Using his brother, Bobby Jr's credit card, David with 2 other family members, purchased a $170 Panasonic radio-cassette player at a store close by. It would be among David's possessions when he died.

The two men spoke for about half-an-hour on a wide variety of topics, including politics. David mentioned that while Douglas had enthusiastically embraced the Democratic hopeful for the presidency, Walter Mondale, he himself "wasn't in harness yet." David impressed Heffernan as being a-political.

"He was politically astute, but not personally involved," Heffernan said, who today lives in Indonesia as a magazine publisher. He thought David looked a bit downcast with a lot on his mind. "He wasn't bubbling," Heffernan thought as he observed David. "Maybe he was a bit melancholy."

It was also on the Friday morning that David started asking around for where he could buy cocaine. He apparently succeeded in finding his connection. A man introduced himself as David Dorr and said that the two of them had met from his time working as Ethel's gardener in 1977. Kennedy did not remember the man. Dorr told David that he was finishing up his job as a bellhop at the Brazilian Court in a few days, but would be around regularly in the meantime. David would also have been able to obtain drugs from other sources.

"If he had a habit before and he knew how to score it," says police Lt Thomas M. Perry, "he would certainly know how to score it anywhere." Charles Hamilton agreed. "David could easily have bought high-quality cocaine in any quantity he wanted. He would be aware of how to get it."

He was later seen at Doherty's, a popular pub just around the corner from the hotel, in the late afternoon. Located on the corner of Royal Palm Way and Country Road in the historic Palm Way building, it had an up-market feel to it and catered to a well-heeled clientele. Today, Amici's, an Italian restaurant operates from the building.

As he began to slake his thirst, that fragile sobriety was soon washed away in a torrent of vodka. Shaun Donnelly, a barman at Doherty's says, "He could really slam 'em back, double vodkas on the rocks," he recalled. "He'd drink that much and it wouldn't show...He'd drink three or four doubles an hour," attested Donnelly. "You try and slow him down. Anybody who drinks double vodka on the rocks is out for a purpose." He met 24 yr old Leslie Griffin from Greenwich, Connecticut here and arranged a date for the following night.

David and Douglas had dinner at the family estate on Friday night. Rose collapsed at the dinner table as paramedics rushed to the scene David was said to be particularly upset by his grandmother's situation.

Following dinner, David with his brother and friend headed out to Chuck and Harold's, a restaurant and nightspot. With a history dating back to the 1920s, its casual, laid back style coupled with alfresco dining and live entertainment, made it a favorite hangout for David when he was in town. He ran into family friend, artist Bob Driscoll who was known for his coastal and harbor scenes, several of which hang in the JFK Presidential Library.

Driscoll watched David and thought he was consuming soft drinks judging by the quantity he was putting away. "I thought it was Perrier water," the artist stated. "But I found out later it was vodka.

"He did look alert to me though," the artist observed. "If he had been drinking (excessively) he would have felt bad. He sure didn't look it to me."

He arrived back at the Brazilian Court sometime later in the evening where he continued to set a frenetic pace. "He planted himself on a barstool and drank up a storm," the barman who served him stated. In the genteel surrounds, the young man stood out not just for his overindulgence. The hotel's clientele tended to be older and sedate, making David's relative youth a focal point, but few recognized him as a Kennedy. While he arrived feeling he could walk about largely incognito, word soon spread that the young man had produced a credit card bearing the Kennedy name. His cover was blown.

"He was very visible going in and out of the hotel over the weekend," Gerald Beebe said. "But he was quiet and no one suspected any problems…"

He wasn't going anywhere on Friday night however. He was "downing vodka after vodka until eventually he started signaling for drinks because he just couldn't talk anymore," a waiter observed. "Before he became incoherent," the waiter furthered, "David was offering cocaine to the bartender, the waitresses and other people drinking at the bar. On at least three occasions he offered pills around. He was taking pills himself, washing them down with the vodka."

"It was very embarrassing," the waiter continued. "The customers and staff alike turned their backs on him. It was a tragic sight. He staggered out of the bar just after 1 a.m. and the last I saw of him he was weaving his way toward his suite."

SATURDAY APRIL 21

His routine quickly became familiar. Hotel maid Carlee Moore was assigned to clean David's room. "Most days he seemed to get up (late)," she says.

Elizabeth Barnett agreed. "David liked to sleep late and would pick up his messages (at the front desk) or we would call them through."

"His brother Doug would always ask him to go to the beach," another hotel maid said. "He said he would rather sleep in."

While his room was messy, Moore didn't observe anything that was unusual in it. "It was typically a boy's room," she thought, observing various items of clothing having been casually discarded. "David has his swimming trunks on every time I saw him," she added. His attire would remain pretty much unchanged - cut off denim shorts with t-shirts or a long-sleeved, button down shirts. When footwear was required, he would wear a pair of Nike sneakers.

After a quick bite to eat, he would either go for a swim or relax by the pool and then imbibe on a few afternoon cocktails poolside. His dinner arrangements either involved a date or family members then he'd hit the bars at night. Mostly he'd be by himself, but would occasionally be joined by family and friends.

David rose sometime after 10 a.m. and called room service for a breakfast of pancakes and six glasses of freshly squeezed orange juice. At 11 a.m. he is seen walking out to the pool.

"He stretched out on a lounge chair beside a tall blonde girl," a staffer recalled. "They got involved in a deep conversation. David was laughing and the girl was giggling," he said. He then noticed the two leave together. "Shortly after noon the girl stood up, threw a beach towel around her blue bikini and followed Kennedy into his suite."

Before his new companion left, David was visited by a close family friend - a young man - who said he watched TV while David snorted coke. He says the girl left soon afterwards.

At lunchtime, David met with Douglas Moschiano, who arranged for a rental car for the Easter weekend. David decided on a gold four-door dodge which he returned on Monday after taking Doug and his friend to the airport.

At this time, while David was out, Heffernan had lunch with Doug, who told him of his concern about David, "getting his career together." He also believed that "David was the brightest of all the Kennedy children."

David was back at the hotel at 1:30 p.m. where he "phoned room service and ordered three double vodkas and grapefruit juice," a barman recounted.

David spent most of Saturday afternoon around the pool of the Brazilian Court with the younger members of the Kennedy family, who had come for a visit. They noticed the closeness of David and Doug - the elder Kennedy brother still drinking vodka and grapefruit juice while chilling out pool side.

Doug wasn't fooled by his big brother's attempts at subterfuge, but retained his strong bond for his big brother, and godfather.

"He was very attentive and caring to David," Heffernan said of Doug. David's other family members weren't fooled either. They also observed his behavior closely and it caused them concern. They were worried that he was back on drugs too.

The suspicions of the younger ones soon filtered back to the older family members. The Kennedy family had become so concerned in fact, that they had Rose's doctor call St. Mary's in Minneapolis on the Saturday afternoon with their suspicions. Staff there gave referrals to treatment programs in the Palm Beach area.

Doug's friend says that at this time David asked him whether he'd like to try heroin. "He asked me did I want to go and get some smack and I said no, that I didn't do heroin," Evans asserted. "He said to me that the stuff in Florida wouldn't get me addicted."

At 5 p.m. after his cousins had returned to the Kennedy estate, David is seen at the bar, looking somewhat depressed. "Kennedy was slumped over the bar - glassy eyed and staring into space," a barman remembered. He stayed for almost an hour before getting up to get ready for his date with Leslie Griffin.

Shaun Donnelly, from Doherty's Bar and Restaurant, saw David come in shortly before 7 p.m. on the Saturday evening. While he waited for his date to arrive, David sat at the bar alone, keeping his own company and slowly sipped two double vodkas. Donnelly says David was looking "pretty sharp" – clean shaven and washed hair. He was dressed in khaki trousers, a dark polo shirt and cowboy boots.

Leslie Griffin says that over dinner, the two of them had a "very meaningful and sensible talk...He was very sensitive," she said, "and on that night, that Saturday night, he was very coherent." Griffin, a Connecticut native, said David made a positive impression on her.

"He was a sweet, sensitive, caring kind of guy, who was struggling with what he was going through," Griffin thought. She found his behavior to be calm and that he wasn't correctly portrayed by the media. "I would say in defense of David, he wasn't this wild drug addict that everybody kind of made him out to be," Griffin concluded. "I feel he has gotten a very terrible rap. He was a very nice man."

Over their dinner, David brought up the Playboy excerpt controversy which had been a focal point in David's life in one way or another, for the past couple of months. David told Griffin how surprised he was by how much he revealed in the interviews. "I can't believe that I said those things," he told his date.

By 8:30 p.m. David was back at the hotel with Griffin. He spotted Robert Driscoll in the Southern Courtyard where he was displaying his artwork in the elegant surrounds of the hotel. Driscoll called David something of a "kindred spirit. He requested his friend's services.

"Paint me a flower," David said. Driscoll agreed. He painted David a red sea anemone, which took the artist 20 minutes to create. They got to chatting.

"He was a sensitive, fine young man," Driscoll stated. "He seemed to be normal acting. We talked about what he was doing. He said he was registering at Harvard to get his degree. He said he'd been on Methadone and that his sisters were working hard to help him to give drugs up.

"I just wonder if it was all too much for him to handle," Driscoll speculated. "This was a sensitive boy who couldn't measure up to the demands. He was sensitive to his surroundings and a little introverted.

"Here's a kid who deserves something," Driscoll thought as he finished up the painting, which David procured for free. "If anyone else had asked for it, they would have had to pay for it," he said. "David asked for a red anemone because it is a very sexy flower. The girl showed an interest in having the painting, but I told David he must keep the painting for himself. He thanked me and agreed. It became his farewell, his last request." Before parting ways for the night, Griffin invited David to a pool party the following day she was co-hosting at a nearby estate.

The Brazilian Court's pianist, John Williams saw David enter the bar a short time after his date left the hotel and observed his behavior. Whatever coherence David had at dinner soon disappeared when he was by himself.

By 10 p.m. "David was completely out of it, sometimes weaving in his seat," Williams thought. "Since the bar required jackets in the evening, the manager asked him to put one on. So they gave him a plaid sport coat. They had to help him on with the jacket - he was in real bad shape. He couldn't move and he was still drinking."

At this time, a vacationing Catholic priest from Chicago, Father Terry entered the bar with a group of people and struck up a conversation with David.

A hotel insider who was at the bar with David said, "When the priest was told that the young drunk was the son of Robert F. Kennedy, he told David, 'perhaps you'll let me visit with you in the morning.'

"Kennedy nodded his agreement," the source revealed. "He asked Father Terry if he would say mass for him when he came. Then he ordered another double vodka, but couldn't even drink it..."

As the bar closed for the evening, David was helped back to his room. "Two hotel staff members took him by the elbows and walked him back to his suite, where they helped him safely into bed," the source said.

SUNDAY APRIL 22

David emerged before 7 a.m. on Easter Sunday morning looking decidedly worse for wear. Obviously feeling the seedy after-effects of the two previous evenings, he wandered up to hotel cashier, Irene Jacobs, clad only in a pair of shorts.

"All he had on was a pair of blue, washed-out shorts," Jacobs said of the early morning encounter. He asked for David. "I said, 'David who?' and he said he didn't know his name. And he said, 'A bellman...'" Jacobs said she didn't know the unkempt man she had spoken with was the son of Robert F. Kennedy. She thought he was a bum off the street.

"I was looking around, really, for somebody to come in and take him out because our guests do not dress that way, and I thought he had walked in off the street," Jacobs said.

"His hair was dirty and hanging down in his face and he had his head hanging down...I figured there was something the matter with him, but I didn't know what it was...He wasn't drunk, I couldn't smell a thing."

Not finding Dorr, David then went out to the pool and ate cups of fruit for his breakfast. David ran into Father Terry as he ate his food, who promised to do mass for him in a little while.

By this time the family had started becoming more concerned about David's conduct. There was no hiding his resumption of drink and drugs.

"He was drinking most of Saturday," Doug says of his brother. "But by Sunday morning I suspected him to be on cocaine. He was sort of jumpy and paranoid...and licking his lips."

At around 9 a.m. Father Terry got some bread and wine from the hotel kitchen to use for the mass and headed to room 107 where six guests were waiting.

"The curtains were drawn, and the priest laid a white cloth on top of a table," said a person present for the mass. "He laid a gold crucifix on this makeshift altar, used a wine glass for a chalice and said the mass as David knelt by his bed, his elbows resting on the rust-colored bedspread and his hands clasped in prayer. His head was bowed.

"In a symbolic communion the priest broke and shared a piece of bread with Kennedy," the person continued. "As David took it he glanced up into the priest's eyes and there were tears in his own eyes. In that moment there was a look of desperate loneliness on David's face, and his features suddenly took on the look of a lost little boy. He looked miserably unhappy and confused."

Following the mass, the two Kennedy brothers spent the rest of the morning lounging around the pool. David was reading a spy novel by author Robert Ludlum. But the book didn't hold his attention for long as his blond companion from the previous day appeared.

At midday, David and Doug decided they wanted hamburgers and fries for lunch and went to the restaurant.

"They wanted to eat on the restaurant patio," one worker said later. "But the maitre d' said they couldn't stay because they were dressed bummy. So they went to their room and we bought them burgers."

David then went back to the pool. In the early afternoon following lunch, he is seen drinking rum and coke when David Dorr appeared.

"We were lying by the pool and Dorr came out and motioned to David," Doug said, who was by now watching his brother's behavior closely. "They went into a little room by the pool and about 25 seconds later I followed. I went in there because I thought he might be getting coke..."

The two Davids stopped talking as the youngest son of RFK walked into the room. As they went their separate ways, Doug followed his shirtless older brother back out to the pool and confronted him with his suspicions.

"I said, 'What's going on?' and he said, 'Nothing' and then he walked away. I said, 'were you getting any smack?' and he said, 'No, I'm just getting girls from that guy Dorr.'"

David then decided to head out. Shortly after, David is seen at Leslie Griffin's pool party. He ran into his old friend Bob Driscoll.

By that time," Driscoll said, "David had begun to look pretty bad. He was out of it...drinking a lot of vodka. He had been on methadone. He was the wrong person to be drinking."

It was at the party that David met Harriet Crouch. She was a member of a New York opera company in Palm Beach for a recital and was also staying at the Brazilian Court. She would meet up with David the following evening.

He didn't stay long at the party - a couple of hours - before heading to the Kennedy estate to visit briefly with his grandmother. He then headed back to the hotel.

The next sighting of David occurred at around 6 p.m. at the Brazilian Court. He ran into Dennis Heffernan again, and over a couple of drinks, the two men made plans to have dinner later that evening. Heffernan told David that he would grab a quick nap before they ate. Unfortunately, he overslept and missed their arranged dinner. Hotel staff says that David stayed on in the bar for a while listening to a female vocalist then went to the restaurant by himself.

"Early Sunday night he walked into the hotel restaurant alone," said a waiter. "He picked at a salad, gulped down a double vodka, then went straight to the hotel bar where he hardly spoke a word except to order vodka."

At 8:30 p.m. Doug had returned from the estate and the two brothers decided to go out to Doherty's - it was the younger Kennedy's last night in Palm Beach. David ate a late dinner of veal piccata with spinach noodles, says the waitress who served the meal, Kim Waldron. The 23yr-old waitress could see that the drink was starting to show.

"He asked me for a date," she said. "But I said, 'sorry - I've got a boyfriend.' He looked a mess," admitted the blue-eyed blond waitress. She said she didn't recognize the disheveled looking young man, until he paid for his drinks with an American Express card bearing the name Mrs Robert F. Kennedy. He threw Waldron a lame line about being new in town and wanted her to show him around. She declined his offer, she says, because, "I didn't want to be seen by anybody who looked like that."

At around 10 p.m. while Doug made his way back to the hotel, his big brother ventured on alone to Chuck & Harold's. David was considerably more successful with his pick-up lines as one of the two women he meets there, 41-year-old German model Marion Niemann, gives him her number.

Back at the hotel very late on the Sunday night, Derrick Evans overheard David speaking with David Dorr. State Attorney David Bludworth asked Evans what the conversation was about.

"About cocaine," Evans replied. "...David Kennedy asked David Dorr if he could get him some more stuff..."

"Are you sure he said some more?" Bludworth asked.

"Yes, he said 'more,' definitely," Evans said.

Evans also stated that he heard David tell Dorr the cocaine he had sold him was of good quality. Evans also said that before retiring for the evening, David admitted to him having been on cocaine for the previous three days.

MONDAY APRIL 23

He had 48 hours to live. As the temperature and humidity rose into the high 80s (31C), the storm clouds were gathering literally and figuratively. A number of things occurred today that adversely affected David and hastened his slide to death. It was as if circumstances were conspiring against him. There was an argument with his family over his interviews and return to drugs - their reaction particularly upset him. His brother, who had kept a close eye on him, had left to go back to school, leaving him in the hotel by himself. His grandmother's worsening condition was a further source of anxiety.

The accumulated stresses would contribute to his most self-destructive day. Before the sun rose on Tuesday, the man would get through 4 grams of coke (more than an "eight-ball") and half-a-gallon (1.8 litres) of vodka. It would not be a good day. As things started to go pear-shaped, his mood and behavior started to go the same way – south.

The day started, as it had the last few days, shortly after 10 a.m. He immediately rang room service for his favorite breakfast - pancakes and six glasses of orange juice. He managed to get it together enough to drive himself and Doug to the estate for lunch.

Rose had collapsed twice during the Easter weekend and priest was on standby to administer last rites if necessary. David and Doug saw their grandmother in her upstairs bedroom. Teddy's son Patrick and Doug's school friend Derrick Evans were also present.

"We just went in and said hello to everyone who was there," Evans remembered. "Then we went upstairs to see David's grandmother. I remember I was by the door...We stayed just a short time."

Staff at the estate noticed some time after the young men had visited that a vial of Demerol, prescribed for Rose, had disappeared. While most immediately assumed David was responsible, he was under the family's constant observation, thwarting his ability to lift the powerful narcotic. This of course, didn't stop his detractors from the accusations of him stealing drugs from his grandmother's deathbed. He clearly wanted it though. But evidence suggests a female cousin stole Rose's medication on David's behalf. He told her he needed it.

"David seemed fine," Evans said of his personal condition. "But he was very upset over how sick his grandmother was. He had never seen her in that bad a condition before."

Housekeeper Nellie McGrail saw David as he visited with his grandmother. "David ran out of the room," she remembered. "He was heartbroken. It was a shock to see her in that condition because he hadn't seen her ill like this."

The two Kennedy brothers stayed briefly to say hello to Teddy and other relatives staying at the estate. Ethel, who wasn't at the gathering, said later that David had become abusive and his odd behavior was causing family members great distress.

Some have suggested that his belligerence stemmed from an argument over David's contribution to the devastatingly revealing Playboy article. The family were said to have been critical over his cooperation. It's believed there was also a confrontation over his return to drink and drugs

"Straighten yourself out!" Ted bellowed at David at one point during the face-off. "Don't use drugs while you're here out of respect for your grandmother - and get back into rehab!"

David was very affected by the emotion-charged, disharmonious scene at the estate. Many feel it was the impetus for the acceleration of his drug use, particularly the fatal introduction of the Demerol. His usage escalated as his mood plummeted.

"A concerned family member told David he didn't look well," McGrail recalled. "He said, 'I don't feel well.'" He lay down on a couch and rested for a short time before leaving the house without telling the family staying at the estate. He drove his brother Doug and Derrick Evans to the West Palm Beach airport and saw them off before returning his rental car.

"After he had driven his brother Doug and his friend to the airport on Monday, he was left alone," Robert Driscoll said. "He was depressed and let down after a party-filled few days.

He went to his room alone to go to bed early. Then he pumped himself up (to go out)."

With Doug's departure, the family's anxiety over David increased. Frequent calls from them would be placed with the hotel regarding David. It seemed their concerns were well founded.

Back at the Brazilian Court in the mid-afternoon, hotel bellhops David Dorr and Peter Marchant sold David two bags of high grade, seventy percent pure cocaine - their fifth deal in as many days. They received a $120 ($250 today) check from David. His signature was later confirmed by the crime laboratory. Police later added that David had made a total of five transactions by check with the bellhops during his stay in Palm Beach totaling $640. However, at least one known cash transaction would have propelled his cocaine expenditure to more than $750 ($1600 today).

"Seventy percent pure cocaine is dangerous," said Mike Tucker, a Palm Beach County narcotics detective. "Too much of it could kill you. That cocaine is pretty strong even for someone with a heavy tolerance." He said most street cocaine is closer to fifty percent pure. "Any time you are doing those kinds of drugs," Charles Hamilton said, "the potential for overdose is unbelievable."

"About 4 p.m. he came out to the pool where he was joined by the blond he'd met there on Saturday," a staffer observed. "A half-hour later they went to his suite - and Kennedy phoned for vodka. Once again, he was snorting coke."

A little later on, Dennis Heffernan bumped into David again. He apologized for missing the dinner they had arranged for the previous evening. To make it up, Heffernan invited David to his home for a pasta dinner with his friends that night, but David declined.

"He said he couldn't that he had a date," the hotel owner stated. The two men chatted as they did when they ran into one another. "He talked about going back to school to get his degree," Heffernan said. "He talked about things he wanted to do in business. He was interested in girls. He showed all the signs of being a healthy, right-minded young male. He was a great guest.

"But you could see a lot in his eyes," Heffernan countered. "The kind of horror he had been through as a child. It wasn't a particularly pained look. He just had a sort of sad, haunted look. He didn't appear to be depressed; he didn't appear gleeful either. He was introspective." It was the last time Heffernan saw David alive.

A hotel employee said David was drinking heavily at the hotel bar in the dying hours of daylight before his date with Marion Niemann.

"He must have polished off a quart (1 litre) of vodka in two or three hours," a barman thought. "One hotel staff member said to me, 'This guy is going to kill himself!'"

He asked the barman if any bars had a late closing. He was told the Kenya Club, a dark, African themed bar, a few blocks away in the city's ritzy shopping district, was opened until 3 a.m. The barman said that David spoke of his regret over his co-operation with authors Collier and Horowitz. David told the barman of the rift it had caused with his family.

"His eyes appeared red, like he'd been crying," one customer who was there thought. "And at times he mumbled to himself. Once I heard him say, 'This is it, this is it -screw it all!'" Sometimes he put his arms on the bar and lay his head on them, just staring," another customer said.

At the Rain Dancer steakhouse in West Palm Beach a little later on, David met up with Marion Niemann. Niemann says David was emotional and very depressed. She said David didn't eat much, "just picked at his food and drank seven vodkas."

They went back to David's room at about 9:30 p.m. where a tearful scene unfolded. She listened as David told her about the sadness of his life stemming from his father's death and how he had struggled ever since.

"They were both sitting on the bed and he was telling her about how unhappy he was," Officer Michael Gabrin reported. The officer says she told police that she asked David, "You take some drugs today?"

"Yes," he responded. "I took some cocaine today."

'David," Niemann said. "This is very sad. You are such a nice person, but you make all the people around you unhappy."

"I can't forget when I see my father on television, "he answered tearfully. "I never find peace inside. I've been full of pain."

Niemann told David he needed help.

"Yes," he agreed. "I'm just crying out for help."

David then told her, "Wait here. I'm going to the front desk to pay my hotel bill." Curious timing and a curious comment indeed considering he had no hotel bill to pay. She said she stayed in the room and watched TV in time David was gone. Upon his return, Niemann noticed David carrying a small plastic bag full of "something white like flour," she recalled. He immediately laid out some of the powder, and through a $20 note, inhaled. "I think maybe, it was cocaine," she said. "I had never seen cocaine in front me - never."

"Should you be doing that David? With the way you feel?" She asked.

"It's alright, don't worry," he told her. "I can handle it."

"Where did you get it?" she asked.

"From a bellman," he responded.

She said he then took some pills that he said he needed for sleeping - probably Mellaril. They lay down on the bed and kissed at his request, but, according to Niemann, went no further. She left David's room at about 11 p.m. She tried to phone around midnight to check on him but there was no answer. He had decided to hit the town once again.

He was seen at 11:30 p.m. waiting alone in the courtyard. It's likely he had arranged to be picked up by new companions Harriet Crouch and Peter Marchant before heading out to the Kenya Club.

At the Club where David arrived shortly before midnight, he was indeed seen drinking with Crouch and Marchant. David sat at the far end of the bar, surrounded by black walls and mirrors with red spotlights on mounted animal heads. He was back into the double vodkas while Crouch and Marchant drank beer. Inspired by the stuffed animals staring down at him, David spoke of boar hunting in Pakistan during a trip there in 1976.

Sometime before 1 a.m. on Tuesday the 24th, the last full day of his life, David asked Crouch to join him for some air, the bar was too depressing, he said. Marchant followed them as David suggested they go for a drive. The three of them sat in the front seat of Marchant's car as David produced a cellophane packet of cocaine. David made the comment that "this doesn't look like very much." The three then took turns to snort the cocaine off a polished stone the size of a salad plate. They then returned to the bar.

At around 2 a.m. David started asking Crouch to take him back to his room at the Brazilian Court. It was evident, Crouch said, that David needed her assistance to get there. Asked why, the opera performer responded, "David was rapidly becoming incoherent."

TUESDAY, APRIL 24

At 9 a.m. Paula Scully was heading off to work from the apartment she shared with David in Boston, when the telephone rang. David calling to let her know that he would be home later that day.

"He was planning on coming back home that afternoon," Scully said. "On the telephone it's hard to get a reading of how well people are and it is hard to deal with sentiment. He seemed well though, very well."

They talked for a few minutes about a vacation to the Bahamas scheduled to start in early May, and David said that when he got back home he planned to start going back to his AA meetings.

"He was happy to be thinking of our vacation together," Scully said. "He was a bit lonely after Douglas left. He hated to be alone. But he was thinking about all the things coming up in his life and he was happy...He didn't want to die...he wanted to live. He was planning the rest of his life.

"He sounded perfectly happy, normal, sober," Paula says of David's mindset in his moments of life. She said of her last conversation with David, "I didn't know he was going to die or otherwise I would have talked to him forever." Following the discussion, and perhaps originally getting up for a bathroom break, David then apparently went back to sleep for a few hours.

In the meantime, Douglas Moschiano said that the hotel operator had received numerous calls from David's concerned family members on the Tuesday morning. They complained of finding his phone line constantly engaged. One call that was left for David at reception was from his Aunt Jean Smith, who said he was still welcome to visit his grandmother, despite the drama of the previous day.

Marion Niemann said she also tried to call David on three occasions and also encountered a busy signal. Late morning, at the insistence of concerned Kennedy family members, bell captain Doug Moschiano went to David's room.

"When I got there, there was a 'Do Not Disturb' sign on the door," he said. "I knocked but no one answered. I unlocked the door with a pass key and opened it just a bit. He was sleeping in the bed and the phone was off the hook. I didn't go in. I closed the door and left."

David emerged only after having slept through breakfast and lunch. "When he finally crawled out of bed, he looked terrible," one insider thought. "His eyes were unfocused and glassy. He (immediately) had three vodkas delivered to his suite. His brother Douglas, his friend and the girl he'd met at the pool had all left the hotel. David was alone...alone with his vodka."

David then took a call from Marion Niemann. He told her he wasn't feeling well and that he might lie down by the pool.

Sometime close to 1 p.m. David emerges from his room and decides to meet a friend, Terrence Murphy, whom he had asked to fly down and join him following Doug's departure. There was a light drizzle falling from the heavens as David walked the short distance to the bar. "...I saw him coming through the courtyard and he walked uptown," Moschiano recalled.

"I flew down and met him at a bar called Doherty's...It was about 1 in the afternoon. I walked in looking for David and saw what looked like an old guy nursing a drink, sitting at the bar with his back to me. When I approached him and he turned around, I couldn't believe it was David."

After the two greeted one another, Terrence took a seat next to David and asked him how he fared at rehab. "Oh yeah, it was well worth the money my Uncle Teddy spent on it," he said. Then raising his double vodka on the rocks, he added, "Cheers, buddy!"

Terrence said that David's drinking so early in the day wasn't a good idea, saying it was making him look like an old man.

"I *am* an old man," David remarked, as he lit a Marlboro.

"How's your mom?" Terrence asked.

"Same as always," David said. "Have you heard about this book I'm in?" David then asked, changing the subject. "I spilled my guts to some punk writer," and he was afraid of how his family would react when the book was finally published. "I really did it this time," he said.

Terrence smiled and put his hand on David's shoulder. "Well, there's always tomorrow," he offered.

David stared ahead blankly. "Not always," he said.

David returned to the hotel later in the afternoon and headed out to the pool for yet more drinks. He was seen to have several Scorpions - a potent rum cocktail.

David approached the front desk to cash a $100 check at 4 p.m. He also asked the staff to call him a taxi to take him out to the Kennedy estate.

But there was drama even before he stepped out of the cab. Apparently he got into a verbal disagreement with the cabdriver, Bill Newman over the fare.

"He was completely blown away," Newman recalled. "He didn't even know he was in a cab. I had an argument with him, trying to get my money, but I finally got paid."

Upon arrival, he was refused entry by security who thought him to be drunk or stoned. The disheveled young man slurring his words was dismissed as a derelict and turned away.

"Half an hour later, one of my buddies picked him up at the house and drove him back to the Brazilian Court Hotel," Bill Newman stated.

The second cabdriver had more sympathy for David, whom he felt had been treated harshly. "I feel like they threw him out of that house," he recalled with some bitterness.

Ethel Kennedy, worrying about her son, called Palm Beach lawyer Howell Van Gerbig Jr, a family friend. He said that in the first of four phone calls he received that Tuesday afternoon, Ethel had told him how upset the family members present at Palm Beach had become over David's strange and abusive behavior.

"She was having a very difficult time, the family members were, with David..." he said. "She told me that he had just gotten out of the drug rehab center somewhere in the Midwest...(and) that he was giving family members a difficult time up at the family home."

Asked for his advice on her son, Van Gerbig told Ethel that he thought David should see a private doctor he knew. Calling him back after having spoken to David by phone, Ethel said David was in really bad shape. Van Gerbig said that Ethel had "begged" David to call the lawyer and that he had agreed to have dinner with Van Gerbig that night. Ethel told the lawyer that her son had also agreed to seek treatment yet again.

A source said that in the phone call to David, Ethel had told her fourth born to stay away from drugs. Perhaps sensing David's resolve might be a put on, "She said it was his last chance and that he had to straighten out his act because he brought dishonor to the Kennedy family," the insider said.

"Ethel said, 'We worry about you all the time. I'm praying to God you've got the strength to beat this terrible fascination with drugs.'"

"She didn't know what to do," Van Gerbig said. "He had been very abusive to members of the family and was upsetting them."

"Do you know of any drugs David might be using?" the lawyer asked Ethel.

"Only the prescription Mellaril, a tranquilizer," She responded.

"When I observed that he must certainly be on other drugs," Van Gerbig answered, she said, 'He promised me he stopped doing heroin, but I'm afraid he's lying to me.'

Van Gerbig said Ethel had become "very, very confused" during the conversation. The gravity of the situation had become startlingly apparent.

Another phone call Ethel made during this period of growing concern over David's welfare was to her nephew and later convicted murderer, Michael Skakel.

"When David relapsed, my aunt Ethel called me to see if I could get him into treatment," Skakel asserted. "She insisted that David remain anonymous. I called every place I knew. None had any beds available. I felt desperate. I was sure that if I told them it was for David Kennedy, they'd relent. I knew how dire the situation was. I begged my aunt to let me use the Kennedy name. 'No absolutely not,' she said. 'I'm not going to let him drag this family through the mud again.'"

Meanwhile back at the Brazilian Court, the staff observes David walking into the hotel at about 4:30 p.m. after his aborted trip to the Kennedy family estate. The front desk thinks he is in good spirits, waving to the staff as he passes by. It would be the last time they see him alive.

David Horowitz says he spoke to Kennedy by phone at around 5 p.m. on the Tuesday afternoon. "The day before David died, I spoke to him. I asked him how he felt about his mother never having visited him (in rehab). David broke down and cried. 'Nobody cares about me,' he said."

Cal Scheidegger was David's drug counselor at St. Mary's, and he says he also spoke to David by phone around this time. David told him of the incident at the estate 45 minutes earlier. He confessed to having consumed nine or ten cocktails.

"I was aware of an incredible uproar over David's use of drugs (& alcohol) after his grandmother had had a stroke," Scheidegger said.

Sydney Lawford-McKelvey drove to West Palm Beach airport during the early evening to pick up Caroline Kennedy. She had come to say her final goodbyes to her grandmother. The discussion around the dinner table at the Kennedy mansion that night was not only Rose's parlous condition but the plight of David as well. At the insistence of the older family members,

Caroline and Sydney agreed to go over to the hotel and check on David.

At the same time over at the Brazilian Court David is still in his room making telephone calls. He is still drinking, but it was his drug use that was becoming concerning. In addition to constant cocaine use, he had also begun injecting Demerol into his right groin. Mystery surrounds when he began shooting the opiate derivative, but Tuesday, appears significant. The autopsy report confirming two fresh puncture wounds proves the drugs very late introduction.

His drinking, while certainly substantial today, was less intense than at other times during his final days. The parlous condition he was in at the Kennedy house a couple of hours later is suggestive of the Demerol's usage. It would be a fatal move - the time-bomb had started ticking.

He is seen with two attractive women entering Chuck and Harold's at 6:45 p.m. They sat at a table but ordered only drinks, no food. "He didn't look well," one waiter there thought. "The three of them left after about 45 minutes," he said.

Caroline and Sydney said they were at the hotel looking for their cousin at around this time. After a brief search of the restaurant and a phone call to his room, they left. They appear to have been two ships passing in the night.

After David had failed to keep the dinner appointment with Van Gerbig, the lawyer got in touch with Ethel again. "I called her back that evening and said that what I'd try to do is have breakfast with him in the morning, and go over and get him and see what the situation was..." Van Gerbig said.

"But you see that's what bothers me," Van Gerbig furthered. "I'm thinking that if I had gone over there early in the morning and maybe you know, gotten into his room and gotten him up, but I don't know...I might have been the one who discovered him dead...You've got to remember you're dealing with an argumentative, volatile type of person from what everybody told me about him and I would be intruding...So I decided not to go over."

David arrived back at the hotel shortly before 8 p.m. to make his final drug buy. 51-year-old bellman Robert Lucke, says he was one of the last people to see David alive. Working the 3 –

11pm shift he says he met up with David Dorr on the Tuesday evening of the 24th at the bell station. "David Dorr came up to me one night and he started bragging and boasting that he's going to sell Kennedy drugs," Lucke said. Dorr told him he was going to get the drugs from Peter Marchant who worked over at the Everglades Club.

"He started saying, 'I'm going to sell Kennedy some cocaine. I can't believe I'm selling a Kennedy some cocaine,'" asserted Lucke. "He said he spent his last $150 to get it for him and that he wasn't making a profit on it. He said he saw the kid shaking, he was sick and he needed it."

"If I'm a wino," Lucke said by way of an example, "and you saw me shaking at a bar, and I had to have a drink, wouldn't you buy me one if you had the money? That's what Dorr did ...He did it for mercy."

Lucke insists he tried to dissuade Dorr from providing drugs to Kennedy. "Don't mess with those kids," he allegedly said. "Even if they ain't Kennedys. Don't mess with them."

"I haven't sold drugs in years," Dorr replied. "But I'm selling it to Kennedy because he's sick. Listen, go see if Kennedy is in the bar and tell him I have the dope."

Lucke rang the bar and asked if David was there - he was. Told it was a bellman, David taking the phone, mistook his subject. "Where the hell have you been? What took you so long?"

"This isn't David Dorr, this is Robert Lucke," the bellman answered.

Lucke told David that Dorr had the coke and to meet Dorr in a room located above the hotel's kitchen on the second floor. David then went to the room and met the bellhop, where the drug transaction took place. He was seen at 8 p.m. walking through the courtyard on his way back to his suite. He spoke briefly to some people; it's not known who they were.

Timothy Hagan said he spoke with David by phone sometime later during the evening. Hagan said he spoke with David for almost an hour. "There wasn't any sign of desperation in his voice," he said. "He seemed pretty positive." Hagan refuses to reveal details of the conversation but said, "David would call a lot. It seemed he was making a real effort, trying to get his life in order."

David was on the books as an afternoon checkout, but he unexpectedly failed to keep to his schedule. Why he changed his itinerary remains a mystery. No one hears from David in his final dozen hours, which are shrouded in mystery. Most likely, he wanted to catch up with his cousin Caroline who had just flown into Palm Beach that afternoon. Alternatively, he may have simply decided to rest up after a week of solid partying. It's doubtful he was in any condition to fly anyway. Speculation aside, he was supposed to get back to his mother on his travel plans, but didn't inform her either of his movements.

Ethel became particularly concerned when Paula Scully calls her during the evening asking if David had arrived there. Sensing something wrong, Ethel calls the hotel. He had not checked out, she was told, but was not answering his phone. She calls several times, one at midnight. "Room 107 please," still no answer.

WEDNESDAY, APRIL 25

At three in the morning, she calls yet again – no response.

First thing in the morning, Ethel calls all of her children asking if they had heard from David. They hadn't. She checks with her sister-in-law Jean Smith, but she and the family still at the estate haven't heard from him since the previous afternoon.

In stark contrast to the panic sweeping through the Kennedy family, the scene at the Brazilian Court couldn't have been more tranquil. With the bulk of the guests having left the hotel, and only 30 of the 117 rooms occupied, the last day of David's life started peacefully.

As with the previous morning, phone calls from the Kennedy family continue to flood into room 107. The phone line was still ringing out without a response.

His frantic mother is still contacting reception at regular intervals without locating her son. "Has he called yet?" Ethel would ask her new assistant, Leah Mason.

"No Mrs. Kennedy."

"Well, where is he?" Ethel asks rhetorically. She tells Mason she's had a premonition that something was terribly wrong with David. "A mother just knows," she said. "I have a terrible feeling."

At 9:45, Ethel calls Caroline Kennedy and asks her to go over and check on David, which she does with her cousin Sydney Lawford-McKelvey. The young women arrive at the Brazilian Court asking for David at 10 a.m. "They phoned David's suite from the lobby but couldn't get an answer," an investigator later stated. "They went to his suite and knocked on the door. They came back and Caroline said that she couldn't get an answer. Then they both left the hotel."

It is suspected that they entered the room and cleaned up before David was discovered. No evidence has yet come to light and it remains speculation. The lead detective on the case Palm Beach police Major Michael Reiter, however, stated in a 1994 interview that he believed the rumors. Palm Beach County Sheriff's resident toxicologist, Jay Pinctacuda found traces of cocaine and Demerol in the toilet bowl and the suspicious lack of drug paraphernalia in the room worried detectives. Police investigators also believed that David's body may have been found naked or semi-naked and was dressed after he died in order to give him some dignity. An anonymous person came forward and said that Sydney had admitted to taking two syringes and cocaine from David's room. Through her lawyer, Sydney vehemently denied this. But serious doubts have remained. "I've never stated this publicly," Reiter said, "but there's a significant likelihood that some evidence was removed."

Additionally, Doug and his friend Derek Evans told police that David kept the key to his room above the molding on the door, allowing easy access to anyone with the knowledge of the key's location. They didn't know whether anyone else knew of the key however.

The motive for a clean-up was clear. Any person or persons having supplied David with the drugs that contributed to his death would have every reason to want to make sure that evidence disappeared.

Back at the estate, Caroline calls Ethel back to say they had been unsuccessful in finding David. They thought he must be out of the hotel. "Well, then where in the world is he?"

Ethel placed another call to Teddy who wondered if he shouldn't fly back down there. But Ethel persuaded him to stay put. At 11:15, Jackie called Ethel after Caroline had told her mother about David going missing. Jackie offered to help in any way she could. One suggestion apparently being the hiring of an investigator. Ethel thanked her and said she would get back to her soon, if they still hadn't located David.

Between the urgent phone conversations, Ethel reflected on an incident nearly a quarter-of-a-century earlier. "I remember when David got the idea to collect sand in little plastic baggies and sell them to tourists as 'Kennedy Sand' for a dollar a bag," she recalled fondly. "Oh, I was so mad at him for that. I wish now I had not been so mad - why was I always so mad?"

At 11:30 a.m. Ethel makes what will be her final call to the hotel. Josephine Dampier, the hotel manager's assistant, took the call. "This is Mrs. Kennedy again," Ethel said. "I'm sorry to keep bothering you, but no one has heard from my son, David. I've called his room repeatedly! My niece was just at your hotel and said that there was no answer at his door. So I need someone to get into room 107 and make sure my boy is not in there." Doug Moshiano, the bell captain and Elizabeth Barnett, the desk clerk, headed to room 107.

As Barnett and Moschiano once again went to check on David's condition, the secretary immediately had a sense of impending doom.

"Douglas and I were standing outside David's door when I had the most ominous feeling," she said. "Call it a mother's gut instinct or whatever, but I knew what we would find." Moschiano too felt uncomfortable, telling Barnett, "Betty, I don't like going in here again."

"There was a 'Do Not Disturb' sign on David's door," Barnett said. "I knocked and there was no answer. I opened the door a little and peeked in, but not all the way, in case he was sleeping. I didn't want to barge in...but I didn't see him." At first, Barnett thought he must have checked himself out.

As they entered the darkened room, they could hear the hum of the air conditioner which was still on. The shades were drawn for sleep. The room was littered with clothes and cans of soda and beer. There was also an empty cigarette packet and a few notes of money on the bed.

On the desk were several items, including a note written on hotel stationary inviting David to Chicago. It was from Father Terry, who had said mass in the room just three days earlier. Also on the desk was a list of phone numbers on another sheet of paper. There were three partially filled drinking glasses on a tray, a shopping bag, and a paperback novel – Robert Ludlum's The Holcroft Covenant, a spy novel. A photo of two women in frames was also among the possessions. A prescription bottle labeled Mellaril was on a small table nearby. A single cowboy boot and a sneaker were on the floor between two foot cushions. A packed green sports bag was also on the floor. Hidden in the wallet was 1.3 grams of cocaine. 15 milligrams was also found on a $20 note on one of the beds, said to have been used by David to inhale cocaine. His telephone was flashing – he had messages.

"No one was on the bed," Elizabeth Barnett commented, "but then I saw David." He was lying slumped between the two beds face down, his head propped against the nightstand. "He looked like he was trying to get to the phone," Barnett thought. He was dressed, as he had been for the past three days, in a pink, long-sleeved, unbuttoned oxford shirt, cut-off denim shorts, brown socks and off-white sneakers. One arm was draped over a silent portable stereo - the one he had bought days earlier. He probably knocked it off the nightstand in an attempt to reach the phone.

"I went over to David and knelt down," Barnett stated, "and touched his leg, I touched his back, and I touched his face. He was cold." She felt David's neck for a pulse - but it was far too late. "There was no doubt the boy was dead." Paramedics on a training exercise nearby were on the scene in only a couple of minutes.

First hand recollections from the attending paramedics seem to indicate that David had been dead for many hours. The coroner however, was not able to pinpoint the exact time of death, but speculated that several hours had elapsed.

Veteran Palm Beach paramedic Chief Ron Perron arrived at David's suite and "saw an obviously dead young man. Rigor Mortis had set in, and his body was stiff and mottling in different colors," He recalled. "His eyes (and mouth) were wide open - staring fixedly with the pupils heavily dilated. They were the eyes of death. You didn't need to be a medical expert to know there was nothing that could be done for him." The paramedics knew their efforts would be futile.

"One of the paramedics attached a cable to his chest from a machine that measures the heartbeat," Perron furthered. "But the machine printout showed only an unbroken straight line.

"The paramedics stared hopelessly at each other," Perron said. "'He's a straight line,' one of them muttered, 'he's gone!'"

Elizabeth Barnett called Josephine Dampier from David's suite and said, "He's gone, he's gone - he's dead!" Dampier, still on the phone to Ethel, told her, "I'm sorry Mrs. Kennedy, we'll have to call you back...we have to get the paramedics."

Ten minutes later Gerald Beebe had the unenviable task of telling Ethel Kennedy her son had died. After taking a moment to gather his thoughts, a staff member dialed Ethel's number, then handed Beebe the telephone.

"Mrs. Kennedy?" he asked.

"Yes," she answered.

"You asked us to check on David. We have called the paramedics and they've arrived."

"I know he's dead, isn't he?" She asked rhetorically.

"Yes, ma'am, he is," answered Beebe.

"She made a mother's sound, a strange sound, like a gasp and said, "oh, dear Jesus, no, no, no!" and hung up the phone...A very distressed mother obviously," he recalled.

By midday, David's cousins Caroline and Sydney were back at the hotel. They emerged from their grandmother's blue and white Cadillac hair still wet and in bathing suits. Sydney cried briefly when told the news but Caroline remained composed. Caroline spent an hour in the manager's office notifying family members.

Journalists shortly after descended on the Brazilian Court Hotel to witness the unfolding of the latest Kennedy tragedy. Within the sea of reporters, the National Enquirer was offering hotel staff $1000 for any inside information.

Police sealed off room 107 for several hours, allowing only a priest to enter, who spent ten minutes with David's body at 2:15 p.m. Kennedy's body was then taken to the medical examiner's office for an autopsy. It was concluded that David had died through "combined drug intoxication." In his bloodstream was cocaine, Demerol and Mellaril. The amounts though were not considered very large. Dr. David Smith, a toxicologist, stated that
it was still possible for the drugs to have proven lethal to someone who had been drug free for some time.

"They're in the abuse range, but not unusually high," he said. "A lot of people die like this in relapse."

In Kennedy's blood the Palm Beach medical examiner found 0.97 milligrams per liter of Meperidine (Demerol), 0.05 mg per liter of cocaine and 0.49 mg per liter of non-Meperidine (Mellaril). The drugs were also found in other parts of the body, leading medical authorities to state that due to testing difficulties, the actual concentrations would likely be higher.

Fresh puncture wounds in the right groin area indicated that he had recently been injecting drugs and was trying to conceal the usage. Bruises, cuts and abrasions on David's head, lips, jaw, neck, chest, abdomen and right arm were also noted in the autopsy. These were put down to the violent convulsions he would have suffered prior to his death. The autopsy also showed that David's lungs were congested and that he had a surgical scar that was said to be a couple of years old. Suicide was ruled out on the basis that David had voluntarily sought treatment on several occasions, indicating that he wanted to overcome his addictions and be well. Though some have disputed it, the conclusion was that death was an accidental drug overdose.

Several medical authorities concluded that David may have lost tolerance to narcotics by going through the detox program at Minneapolis. He may have taken more Demerol than his brain could handle. "One could at least imagine that just coming out of a detox center set him up for a miscalculation," Dr. Lester Grinspoon of Harvard Medical School stated.

Dr. Norman Zinberg another Harvard authority said that drug overdoses among recently detoxified people was well known. "What usually happens," he said, "is that when someone is coming out of detox they're so busy reassuring themselves and others they are going to stay clean, those warnings are hardly heard."

Chris Lawford upon hearing of the tragic news said, "David had been dying for years, but I never thought he would pull it off. Did he just nod off or was there the fear of knowing he wasn't coming back? How could he do this to me? Leaving me alone in my sinking boat no longer with someone closer to the edge than me."

"I learned later that David had died because he was trying to get sober," Lawford furthered. "...For the first time in a while, his system was clean. This is a dangerous time for an addict. We go back to doing what we did before treatment at the same dosage and it's sayonara amigo."

At 7:45 p.m. David's body, covered by a red cloth, was wheeled away from the site of the autopsy on a stretcher. The body was placed in a black hearse with David's eldest brother, Joe II, riding up front. David would spend the night at the funeral home before making his way back to Washington in the morning.

At the same time David's body was on its way to the funeral home, police discovered the 1.3 grams of cocaine hidden in David's wallet.

He would be buried on Friday, April 27th in the family plot of Holyhood Cemetery in Brookline. The tumultuous journey of David Anthony Kennedy was complete.

AFTERMATH

For the two bellhops, Dorr and Marchant, their harrowing journey was only beginning. They were charged with conspiracy to sell cocaine three weeks after David's death. They were both released on a $25,000 bond. Amidst the media spotlight, every snippet of the 13 month investigation was duly noted. Defense attorneys were feeling very confident of a positive result for the former bellhops. They saw 2 major problems for the prosecutors: One was proving that the sold cocaine was the same cocaine in David's body (which was voluntarily ingested). The other issue was that David died of a "combined drug intoxication." It was the effects of the three drugs working together that knocked David over - not any one in particular. In December 1985, the defense lawyers were proven correct. Both men received 18-months probation and a $200 fine (not to mention $30,000 worth of legal bills). They later had the convictions quashed after they successfully completed the good behavior period.

"Unfortunately, I got caught up in the media blitz," David Dorr later said. "It was an incredible swirl of events. Every time I looked up, there was this person in the paper and on the TV with the same name as me. It's like it's not even me. It's like a bad dream." Dorr added that, "I feel in no way was I responsible for David's death. I had to take a plea to end this nightmare. I never bought cocaine in my life. I was aware there was coke in Palm Beach, but I stayed away from it...After all this, I never want to hear about it, I never want to talk about it. In time, people forget - but I'll never forget. Every day that goes by, there isn't one hour where this doesn't flash through my head. It's been a terrible strain."

Ted Kennedy issued a statement upon David's death that spoke poignantly of the loss. It remains the only statement the family has publicly made on his death. "It's a very difficult time for all members of our family, including David's brothers and sisters who tried so hard to help him in recent years. All of us loved him very much. With trust in God, we all pray that David has finally found a peace that he did not find in life."

"He was a troubled young man searching desperately for a meaning to his life," Tim Hagan stated. "Obviously, he just couldn't find it."

Elizabeth Barnett said, "I just remember looking at that boy lying there and thinking, 'Grace of God this could be my boy.' They all say that David was the sensitive one...I don't care how much power you have, how much money. When you are a child like that, you are alone."

"I think it's true what some said that David died the day his father did," Paula said. "His father was his world, and they did things that David could not get from anyone else."

"David was not a bad boy," one mentor of David's thought. "He was a good boy who used drugs because he hurt so much. If only he could have coped with his pain and survived, he would have made a great contribution."

His girlfriend from St. Mary's Rehab said that, "He called me (from Palm Beach) to read a little poem he'd written for me, and I taped it over the phone," she remembered. "It said, 'Roses are red, violets are blue, my mind is right, I already miss you.'

"After I heard he was dead I played the tape again and cried as I heard his voice," she said. "At least now he's with his father - and that was what he wanted."

EPILOGUE: DEATH BE NOT PROUD

The expressions told the story – pained and grimfaced. Members of the Kennedy family prepared to farewell one of their own – twenty-eight-year-old David Anthony Kennedy. It was 8 a.m. on Thursday, April 26, 1984 – David had been discovered dead less than twenty-four hours earlier. At Quattlebaum's Funeral Home in West Palm Beach, four family members (Jean, Caroline, Sydney and Joe II) listened as Rev. Don O'Brien, a priest at St. Edward's Catholic Church, conducted a 20 minute prayer and blessing service. Sydney openly wept.

At 11 a.m. David's coffin encased in a cardboard crate, made the eerily silent journey from the funeral home to a waiting black hearse. The only sounds coming from the clicks and whirs from the reporters cameras. David's brother Joe walked somberly behind the casket. Eastern Airlines flight 790 would fly David back to Washington D.C. with Joe, Caroline and Sydney. They deplaned from an exit separate from the one used by commercial airlines.

At 2 p.m. a black Cadillac hearse and two limousines with several Kennedy family members drove onto the runway and waited for the plane. Four young men in suits stepped out of the limos and stood in a row behind Joe as the casket, packed in a cardboard box with red air freight stickers, was unloaded and placed on a conveyer belt with other luggage.

At the National Airport (later Ronald Reagan Airport), an electrical overload caused a power failure and shut down lights and escalators at the airport. By the time power was restored and the reporters dashed to the gate, David's grey metal casket had been unloaded and placed in the waiting hearse. In death, he had escaped at least some of the attention so often overwhelming to him in life.

Mid-Afternoon a hearse, followed by 2 limousines, pulled into the driveway of Hickory Hill. David's mother Ethel dressed simply and elegantly in a black dress and pearls, had visited the grave of RFK with several other family members for 20 minutes at lunchtime.

Eight young men wearing white shirtsleeves and ties helped carry David's coffin into Hickory Hill. Ethel and Teddy walked slowly behind, followed by other family members on a beautiful sun-splashed afternoon.

The private wake got under way in the late afternoon as reporters, photographers and TV cameramen clustered outside along the Chain Bridge Road address eager for a peak of proceedings. Inside, a peaceful calm seemed to envelop the gathered mourners, numbering about 40. They strolled on the lawns, and took turns swinging gently in a tree swing at the back of the house. Several relatives stroked horses stabled on one side, dogs played and birds chirped in the trees.

Time magazine captured the mood and atmosphere of the occasion:

"*Babies squealed, dogs tore around among the guests, bounding onto the furniture. Two Roman Catholic priests circulated among the people. Ethel bore up stoically. She spent much of her time with David's coffin in one room of the house. David's brothers were close to tears, but perhaps they remembered their grandfather's hard rule: 'Kennedys don't cry.'*"

People talked in small groups, hugging, often crying, and occasionally laughing. "It had the pastoral feeling of an outdoor wake on a beautiful day," said one man who attended. "There was something timeless about the day, something both tragic and exquisite." But he said there was no talk of what might have been. "After all," he said, "this had been going on for 10 years or more. We all had little remembrances of David – nice ones – and we talked about them. But there was no one who felt he could saved David."

David's eldest brother found it difficult to fathom how David could have felt so unloved by the family. "If only David had known how much we loved him," Joe sad sadly. "But I don't understand how he didn't know it. That's just who we are, especially the brothers. I mean, who is closer than the Kennedy brothers? The thing we have, only we brothers understand it, and we just always know it's there. I just don't understand how he didn't know it. I just don't..."

Another grieving brother said, "I wish we had handled all of it differently. But I don't know what else we could have done."

Lance Morrow wrote in time:

"That night the wake had some gaiety about it. The buffet tables were heaped with ham, turkey, macaroni casserole, tomato aspic and lasagna. David's coffin stood in the drawing room. The guests reminisced about David's brighter sides. Ethel was composed, perhaps because, as a friend says, 'she believes he went right up there with his father.'"

Friday morning, April 27th dawned and with it saw a private mass where 75 family and friends had started gathering on the lawns of the RFK estate early in the morning. Among the early arrivals were Ted Kennedy, George McGovern, Art Buckwald and Jackie-O. The strains of "Alleluia" could be heard emanating from within the grounds welcoming the guests as they arrived. Later, a 15 member youth choir rang out across the rolling hills of Hickory Hill with Beethoven's "Ode to Joy" as the life of David Anthony Kennedy was celebrated. It was a warm, tranquil spring day, seemingly devoid of much of the turbulence that marked David's short life.

Historian Arthur Schlesinger attended the funeral mass and wrote later in his journal about the poignant day. "I attended David Kennedy's funeral mass yesterday. It was held on the terrace at Hickory Hill – a lovely day, fragrant with spring, the deep green grass rolling away toward the swimming pool and tennis court. I thought of all the happy times I have had through the years at Hickory Hill and the sad times too. The younger brothers read prayers; Kathleen spoke charmingly about David, so did Ted Kennedy choking back tears...Ethel was composed, pale, rather beautiful. It was a profoundly sad occasion."

The cover of the program was a letter David, then 12 years old, had sent his mother after Bobby's death – the Donne quotation, "Death be not proud..." carefully written and decorated – heartbreaking.

At 11:15 a.m. the gates open and the hearse carrying David's body drove out of the estate on its way to Dulles Airport for the final journey. Sun streamed into the windows of the car putting a spotlight on the white roses and baby's breath sitting on top of the casket. He was escorted by six motorcycle policemen and several Fairfax County squad cars on the 30 minute trip to the airport.

The privately charted plane landed at Boston's Logan Airport shortly before 1:30 p.m. as David's brothers and cousins once again had the task of unloading his coffin and bearing his weight to the hearse. Security once again very tight, with plainclothes policemen arriving at Brookline's Holyhood Cemetery by 1 p.m. a full hour before the burial services were scheduled to begin. Everyone in the cemetery was asked to leave.

The limos and private cars containing about 45 of David's family and friends duly arrived. The blue hearse carrying David pulled up and his brothers Joe and Bobby Jr got out from the front. A white canvas enclosure on Cushing Knoll, where the family plot was located, flapped gently in the spring breeze. Through their tears, mourners placed wreaths and bouquets of flowers on David's simple wooden coffin. Eight white floral arrangements were set in baskets and arranged in front of the six-foot high, seven-foot wide granite memorial bearing the name "Kennedy" and marking the back of the plot.

Boston Archbishop Bernard F. Law and the Rev. John F. Fitzgerald, a Kennedy cousin, known as "Father Jack", led the 20 minute graveside service. 100 onlookers, photographers and reporters waited by the front gate, about 200 metres away unable to hear the words, though the archdiocese later furnished a partial text.

Archbishop Law, robed in purple and white, sang in Latin the hymn, "Salve Regina" the beginning of which translates" "Hail, holy queen mother of mercy, our life and sweetness, and our hope! To you do we cry, poor banished children of Eve; to you do we send up our sighs, mourning and weeping in this valley of tears."

"Let us pray for our brother to our Lord Jesus Christ, who said, 'I am the resurrection and the light. The man who believes in me will live even if he dies, and every living person who puts his faith in me will never suffer eternal death,'" the Archbishop told the gathering.

"Lord hear our prayer," the family and friends repeated before reciting the Lord's Prayer. David's coffin, visible in the fading sunlight, was then lowered into the earth.

"Understandably, it was a very emotional service," said the family spokesman. "There were several prayers said by the entire group, the entire family. It was somber…There were obviously tears. People did show their emotions."

Also present among the mourners was David's academic advisor at Harvard, John Marquand, with whom he had become very close in the preceding 6 months. He said, "There was a great sense of personal loss."

The final word on David Anthony Kennedy is best summed up by a friend whose life he touched and helped at a time when his own was in turmoil.

"He was an important person in my life, it was for such a short time, but his touch in my life still reverberates," she told this author in 2009.

"I think the fact that he made friends and kept friends the way he did, speaks volumes of his character. His perseverance gives insight into the man, the man who seemingly, could not get it together, and yet, helped so many. He was with us for such a short time, 28 years, but his memory will forever be etched in the hearts of those who knew him and loved him."

© Grahame Bedford / davidanthonykennedy.com 2006

APPENDIX: TRIVIA

- The first RFK offspring to be born via caesarean section
- Born and died on a Wednesday
- 6'2" (188 cm) and 160 pounds (73 kg)
- Spoke with a lisp
- Youngest person to climb Mount Rainier in 1969 – aged 14 years
- His income 1980-84 was about $35,000 per year ($90,000 today)
- Often wore his father's shoes
- In the early 1980s had three Nancy's in his life
- Had a special affinity with sex Goddess Marilyn Monroe
- Between 1976-1979 had 2 overdoses, 3 arrests, 4 stints in rehab, and 5 hospitalizations
- At the time of his death, added another arrest, 2 o.d's and 2 more stints in rehab
- Sold Amway products in Sacramento, Ca
- Disliked cats
- Was a compulsive lead-foot with numerous vehicle related incidents: 1 accident, 1 DWI (driving while intoxicated) and at least 6 traffic violations
- Drove a green-colored BMW sports coupe
- Was a published journalist at 18 (Nashville Tennessean)
- Broke his right arm at 13 and his left leg at 23
- Received his broken arm from Ray Schoenke, Washington Redskins lineman
- Rented his first apartment in New York at East 72nd Street
- In his adult years, lived in Sacramento longer than anywhere else (two-and-a-half years)
- His last residence was at Beacon Street, Beacon Hill, in Boston.
- Favorite breakfast was cinnamon pancakes with freshly squeezed orange juice
- David was a smoker – Marlboro being his brand of choice.

BIBLIOGRAPHY

BOOKS
Adler, B. The Kennedy Children: Triumphs and tragedies. London. Franklin Watts, 1980.
Burke, R.E. The Senator: My Ten Years with Ted Kennedy. London: Sidgwick & Jackson, 1992.
Collier, P. & Horowitz, D. The Kennedys: An American Drama. New York: Summit, 1984.
Horowitz, D. Radical Son: A Generational Odyssey. New York: Free Press, 1997.
Heymann, C. RFK: A Candid Biography. London: William Heinemann, 1998.
James, A. The Kennedy Scandals and Tragedies. Lincolnwood: Publications International, 1991.
Kennedy, E.M. True Compass: A Memoir. New York: Twelve, 2009.
Kennedy-Lawford, C. Symptoms of Withdrawal: a Memoir of Snapshots and Redemption. New York: Harper Collins, 2005.
Leamer, L. Sons of Camelot. New York: Harper Collins, 2004.
Lowe, J. A Time Remembered. London: Visual Quartet, 1983.
Oppenheimer, J. The Other Mrs. Kennedy. New York: St. Martin's, 1994.
O'Sullian, M. & Shpritz, D. Palm Beach: Then and Now. Palm Beach, FL: Lickle Publishing, 2004.
Patterson, M. Searching For the Impossible: the Quest to End All Addiction. Lesmahagow, Scotland: The Long Rider's Guild Press, 2006.
Rainie, H. & Quinn, J. "David in Exile", Growing up Kennedy: the Third Generation Comes of Age, p.187-1991. New York: Berkley Books, 1983.
Schlesinger Jr, A. Robert Kennedy and his Times. New York: Ballantine, 1978.
Skakel, M. Dead Man Talking: A Kennedy Cousin Comes Clean. Book proposal.
Slevin. J. & Spagnolo, M. Kennedys: the New Generation. Bethesda, MD: National Press Books, 1990.

Taraborrelli, JR. Jackie, Ethel, Joan: Women of Camelot. New York: Rose Books, 2000.

Taraborrelli, JR. After Camelot: a Personal History of the Kennedy Family 1968 to the Present. New York: Rose Books, 2012.

MAGAZINES, JOURNALS AND NEWSPAPERS

Achenbach, J. "The Curse Has Followed the Clan." The Miami Herald, April 26, 1984, p.1A.

Achenbach, J. "Autopsy Finds Needle Marks on Kennedy." The Miami Herald, May 25, 1984.

Achenbach, J., Hoffman L. & Marcus, D. "David Kennedy's Death Ended Pain." The Miami Herald, October 13, 1984, p.A1.

"A Kennedy Writes of Hopeless Addiction." St. Petersburg Independent, May 3, 1984, p.2A.

"After a Year, Ethel Kennedy Remains the Spirit Raiser." Fresno Bee, May 25, 1969, p.74 & 78.

Altoona Mirror, May 2, 1984.

Associated Press. "Kennedy Youths Escape Injury in Accident: Girl Badly Hurt." Greeley (Colorado) Tribune, August 14, 1973.

Associated Press. "Kennedy Accident: Paralysis Feared as Crash Aftermath." Portsmouth Herald (NH), August 15, 1973, p.13

Associated Press. Judge Fines Kennedy in Auto Crash." Newport Daily News, August 20, 1973, p.13.

Associated Press. "David Kennedy Gets 2 Fines." News Journal Mansfield, February 18, 1977.

Associated Press. "RFK's Son 'Robbed' in Harlem Hotel." Daily Herald, September 7, 1979, p.1.

Associated Press. "Robbed? Say RFK Son – Sought 'Coke'" The Post Standard, September 7, 1979, p.1.

Associated Press. "David Kennedy Had Life of Tragedy, Hope & Drugs." Chronicle-Telegram, April 26, 1984. P.A4.

Associated Press. "Hagan: 'Kennedy in Good Spirits.'" Chronicle-Telegram Elyria, April 27, 1984, p.A4.

Associated Press. "'He's Dead Isn't He?' Ethel Asked." Chronicle-Telegram Elyria, April 27, 1984, p.A4.

Associated Press. "Kennedy Bellhop Sought to End Nightmare." Miami Herald, December 8, 1985, p.3.

"A Stone Throwing David in Trouble." News Journal, Mansfield, May 3, 1968, p.3.
Ayres Jr. B. Drummond. "A Troubled Kennedy Makes His Last trip Home." New York Times, April 27, 1984, p.A1 & B6.
Barnicle, M. "A Gentle Soul Despite it All." Boston Globe, April 27, 1984.
Bradlee, B. Jr. & Lehmann, B. "David Kennedy Found Dead in Florida Hotel." Boston Globe, April 26, 1984.
Cafarell, K. "Son of Robert Kennedy Among Six Injured as Vehicle Flips off Road." UPI, August 14, 1973.
Carlson, P. "David A. Kennedy 1955-1984: RFK's Fourth Child Eased the Pain of his Father's Death with Drugs & Drink, But the Prescription Proved Tragically Fatal." People Weekly Magazine, May 14, 1984.
Cass, J. "Relatives Take Kennedy's Body Home." Philadelphia Daily news, April 27, 1984.
Courier, May 9, 1984.
Cheshire, M. "David Kennedy's Constant Counselor." The Washington Post, January 22, 1980, p.B1.
Chronicle Staff. "Kennedy: 'Clean, Dry Life Boring." Chronicle-Telegram, Elyria, May 2, 1984.
Courier Staff. "Efforts in Vain." Waterloo Courier, March 17, 1980, p.9.
Christie, M. "The Authors Have Their Say." Boston Globe, June 21, 1984.
Daniel L. "In Death, He Looked Like a Little Boy." Syracuse Herald American, April 29, 1984, p.A1 & A10.
Daily Herald Staff. "Last Days of Young Kennedy: Saddened by his Visit to Matriarch." Tyrone Daily Herald, June 7, 1985.
Enquirer Staff. "David Kennedy: The Real Story – His Shocking, Tormented Last Five Days." National Enquirer, May 15, 1984, P.30-35.
Donovan, K. "Mystery Girl Can't Shed Any Light on David Kennedy's Death." Victoria Advocate, May 1, 1984.
Globe Staff. "The Affluent Addict: a Treatment Dilemma." Boston Globe, January 1980.
Herald Staff. "Cashier in Hotel Details Meeting With Kennedy." The Miami Herald, May 24, 1985, p.8.

Hoffman, L. & Marcus D. "Tragedy Again Hits the Kennedys: RFK's Son David, 28, Dies in Palm Beach." The Miami Herald, April 26, 1984.
Holmberg, D. "Tests Set in RFK's Son's Death." Philadelphia Daily News, April 26, 1984, p.3.
"Investigator: David Kennedy Wrote Check to Bellhop." Daily Intelligencer, December 12, 1984.
Jacobs, J. "Robert Kennedy Jr Wants a Career in Public Service." Winnipeg Free Press, August 26, 1978.
"Kennedy in Intensive Care." Winnipeg Free Press, April 28, 1978, p.5.
"Kennedy probe asks for Connecticut Woman's Help." Boston Globe, May 18, 1984.
Langner, P. "Kennedy's Psychiatrist Fined on Drug Count." Boston Globe, January 19, 1980.
Lawlor, J. & Price, D. "A Hard, Hard Time is Over." Philadelphia Daily News, April 26, 1984.
Lehman, B. "Outside Suite 107, Questions Linger." Boston Globe, April 26, 1984.
Lehman, B. "Kennedy's Body Taken to Virginia." Boston Globe, April 27, 1984.
"Lee Students at State Olympics." Kingsport Times, June 12, 1974, p.11.
Lescaza, L. "RFK Son Robbed at Site Known for Drug Activity." Washington Post, September 7, 1979, p.A3.
Lescaza, L. "David Kennedy Enters Boston Hospital." Washington Post, September 13, 1979.
Marin, V. "Kennedy Death Probers Arrest Two Bellhops." The Gettysburg Times, May 17, 1984.
Moran, E. & Morrison, J. "He Feared RFK Would be Shot Like His Uncle John." Philadelphia Daily News, April 27, 1984.
"Newsmakers: David Kennedy." The Lima News, April 17, 1976.
"Political Horizons." Parade, August 24, 1977, p.20.
Morrow, L. "The One Caught in the Undertow: David Anthony Kennedy." Time Magazine, May 7, 1984.
Newsweek Staff. "Again, Death in the Family." Newsweek, May 7, 1984.
New York Daily News Staff. "Kennedy: 'clean, dry life boring.'" Chronicle-Telegram, May 2, 1984. P. A6.

Noyes, L. "Memories of a Childhood Friend." Boston Globe, April 28, 1984.

Orlando Sentinel, 6/9/85, UPI.

Palm Beach Daily Herald, 4/26/84-4/28/84.

Palm Beach Daily News, 4/26/84-4/28/84.

People Staff. "Friends and Family Rally Around David, the Bright and Troubled Kennedy Rebel." People Weekly Magazine, September 24, 1979.

People Staff. "Ethel Kennedy, a Brave Front, Fought to Maintain a Dynasty and a Home." People Weekly Magazine, May 14, 1984.

Petacque, A. Chicago Sun Times, 4/26/84.

"Pictures released of room where David Kennedy died." Chronicle Telegram, Elyria, Ohio, February 13, 1985, p. D8.

Pienciak, R. UPI, 10/13/84.

Post Staff. "Keeper of the Clan: the Tough Warm Love of Ethel Kennedy." Washington Post, June 4, 1981.

Quindlen, A. "The Kennedy Who Went Wrong." McCalls, April 1980.

Raab, S. "Police Officials Explain Action in Kennedy Case." New York Times, September 8, 1979, p.24.

Rainie, H. "Kennedy's Friend Says That He Was Planning His Life." New York Daily News, May 4, 1984.

"Remembering JFK." The Argus, May 30, 1977, p.16.

"Report Says that David Kennedy Was Turned Away From Estate." Boston Globe, October 25, 1984, p.3.

"RFK's Son Caught Throwing Rocks." The Port Arthur News, May 3, 1968, p.9.

"Robert Kennedy's Son, 20, is Held on Speeding Charge." New York Times, July 14, 1975, p.14.

"Senator Sought to Rush Probe of David's Death." The Daily Herald, October 25, 1984.

Sheehan, S. "Part 1: Ethel is Determined to be Brave." Independent Press Telegram, Long Beach, CA, November 30, 1969.

Sheehan, S. "Part 2: Ethel Has Money and Spends it." Independent Press Telegram, Long Beach, CA, December 1, 1969.

Sheehan, S. "Part 3: Ethel Takes Her Role of Mother of 11 Seriously." Independent Press Telegram, Long Beach, December 2, 1969.

Sheehan, S. "Part 4: Friends Say Ethel's Sense of Humor Full of One Liners." Independent Press Telegram, Long Beach, December 3, 1969.

Sontag, D. "To His Children, RFK Still Looms Large." South Coast Today, June 22, 1997.

Star, May 15, 1984, p.17 & p.37.

Stephenson, M. "David Kennedy Charged With Reckless Driving." The Lima News, July 23, 1975.

Stuart, R. "Robert Kennedy's Son David Found Dead in Hotel." New York Times, April 26, 1984, p. A1 & D23.

Sugar K. "Final Days in Plush Hotel." The Alton Telegraph, April 26, 1984, p. A16.

Sylva, B. "I'm Pretty Much of a Regular Guy." Sacramento Bee, August 27, 1982.

Sylva, B. "RFK's Troubled Son David, Dead at 28: Young Kennedy Found Quiet Haven in Capital." Sacramento Bee, April 26, 1984.

Thornton, M. "Drug Traces Found in Kennedy's Body." Washington Post, April 27, 1984.

Thornton, M. "Kennedy Chronicles." Washington Post, June 14, 1981. P.B1.

"Toxicologist says drug dosage Kennedy took wasn't unusual." Syracuse Herald Journal, May 28, 1984, p. A5

"Traces of drugs were found in David Kennedy's bathroom." New York Times, October 17, 1984, p. A17.

Treaster, J. "David Kennedy Listed as 'Very' Seriously Ill With Heart Infection." New York Times, September 13, 1979, p.B1.

Trebble, A.L. "Style, Personalities." Washington Post, July 29, 1980, p.C2.

"Two in Harlem Rob David Kennedy, 24 Year Old Son of Late Senator." New York Times, September 6, 1979, p. D21.

UPI. "David Kennedy Fined $50 in Traffic Case." The News (Van Nuys), September 28, 1975.

"David Kennedy Seen as Designated Sick One." Salina Journal, April 29, 1984, p.24.

"Kennedy Youth Hospitalized." Chronicle-Telegram, March 24, 1976.
UPI. "RFK Son has Pneumonia." The Argus, March 26, 1976.
UPI. "RFK Son Undergoes Surgery." The Argus, April 17, 1976, p.14.
UPI. "A Kennedy is Arrested." The Times Herald, January 31, 1977, p.16.
UPI. "Kennedy Clan Mom on David." Daily Herald, September 8, 1979.
UPI. "David Kennedy Ran Away From Home: Reports." Daily Herald, September 12, 1979.
UPI. "Heart Valve Infection Slows David Kennedy." Daily Herald, September 13, 1979.
UPI. "David Kennedy Discharged From Hospital." Chronicle-Telegram, October 26, 1979.
UPI. "Lee B. Macht, Harvard Professor and Leader in Mental Health Field Dies." April 29, 1981.
UPI. "David Kennedy's final days: drugs, vodka and depression." Philadelphia Daily News, October 13, 1984.
UPI. "David Kennedy Never Outgrew Boyhood Horrors." Sunday Telegraph, April 29, 1984, p. 1 & p.8.
UPI. "Kennedy autopsy says death was accidental." New York Times, May 25, 1984, p.14.
UPI. "Papers: son's actions scared Ethel Kennedy." Miami Herald, May 18, 1985, p.A1.
"Who is in the News: Kennedy." The Independent, April 26, 1976.
White, T. "The Wearing Last Weeks and a Precious Last Day." Life, June 21, 1968.

WEBSITES
http://www.census.gov/hhes/www/income/4person.html
http://www.davidanthonykennedy.com
http://thekennedys.conforums3.com/
http://en.wikipedia.org/wiki/Sacramento_California

Interviews conducted in 2009 with confidential sources

Printed in the USA
CPSIA information can be obtained
at www.ICGtesting.com
CBHW021916121024
15709CB00031B/278